OFFSCRIPT

RECIPES FOR SUCCESS

LARRY J. NAMER

Offscript

Recipes for Success

Larry J. Namer

Copyright © 2025

All rights reserved.

ISBN 979-8-9896793-9-3

Joint Venture Publishing

The Millionaire Mentor, Inc.

Printed in the United States of America

TABLE OF CONTENTS

FOREWORD

The word "can't" has long been the demise of many a dream. After all, if there is a firm belief that something is impossible, most people will not even try. Either that, or they'll give in at the first sign of criticism, skepticism, or negativity that is thrown their way.

Those who give in and give up easily are, unfortunately, the majority.

Thankfully, Larry Namer is in the minority.

Larry is the poster child for the person least likely to become the greatest media and entertainment mogul of our time. But Larry defied the odds and refused to take no for an answer. He didn't know that what he wanted to do was unheard of, so he refused to give up. And by pressing forward, he changed the entertainment world as we know it.

For over a decade, Larry and I have been more than friends; we've become alliances in creativity and ambition.

Together, we've navigated challenges, celebrated victories, and fueled each other's passions. Our journey is a testament to the power of collaboration and unwavering support—the same characteristics Larry brings to his professional relationships around the world.

Like its author, this book is unapologetically authentic. It's a one-of-a-kind journey toward becoming an international media and entertainment mogul—against the odds and despite those who told him it couldn't be done.

If Larry Namer, an assistant underground cable splicer from Coney Island can do the unthinkable, so can you. Just follow his recipe for success (and don't forget to try the other delicious recipes he shares in this book—you'll be glad you did!).

To your success,

Greg S. Reid
Bestselling Author and Founder of Secret Knock

CHAPTER 1

WEST 29TH STREET: FAMILY, FOOD, AND FUN

How does someone go from being an underground assistant cable splicer to the top of the international media and entertainment corporate ladder?

I'm here to tell you that it's been quite an incredible journey, and it all started in the hood, otherwise known as Coney Island, Brooklyn, New York. The Coney Island I grew up in was more than the boardwalk, amusement park atmosphere that it was known for. In reality, it was an impoverished and rough area, though we didn't realize that at the time because it was all we ever knew. The Joneses we aspired to keep up with were, in fact, just as poor, so we figured our life and town were normal. In other words, we didn't know any different.

Imagine the culture shock when the young man who worked under New York City's streets found himself in the throes of the entertainment capital of the world. I don't know if Hollywood was ready for me, but somehow my upbringing and life had prepared me for "Hollywood." I say Hollywood with the understanding that it is no longer the geographic center of the entertainment world, but rather the measure of creativity and quality.

And it all started generations before I was born. My father's family came from Spain way back but moved to Turkey. Most of them then migrated to Cuba and South America because they spoke Spanish, but my grandfather chose to move to New York City and eventually ended up in Coney Island, where my dad and his seven siblings grew up. Raising eight kids isn't easy, and during the depression, times got really tough during the depression. Unfortunately, my grandparents found that they weren't able to take care of all of their kids anymore, so my dad was sent to a children's home, where he stayed until he was reunited with his family as a teenager.

While my father spoke to his parents and siblings in Spanish, he wanted his kids to be raised as Americans through and through and he refused to speak Spanish to us or even in front of us. My parents were proud to be American and were quite patriotic and willing to do whatever was necessary for their country. When World War II broke out, my mom worked in the war manufacturing effort in Brooklyn, and my father enlisted and served in a tank unit in Northern Africa and Italy until he was wounded in the line of duty. To this day, I still have his Army canteen and his purple heart, and I am proud of the service and sacrifice he gave for his country.

Because my grandfather had Parkinsons disease, I don't have as many memories of him as I do the rest of the family; however, I recall visiting and often seeing him propped up in a chair. On the other hand, I knew my grandmother on my dad's side very well. On my mom's side, we all lived in the same four-family building, with my grandmother living in the apartment upstairs and my Aunt Fanny residing in the apartment next door to us. We lived in a two-bedroom apartment across the hall, with one bedroom being for my parents, and my sister, Harriet, and I shared the other bedroom.

The fourth apartment was rented to Mrs. Markowitz, who was not related to us, but it sure seemed like she was. As you can see, my mom truly had the proverbial village to help her raise us kids. That village went beyond the four-family house we lived in and even encompassed our neighbors. This was back in the day when kids were free to roam, and parents weren't worried because everyone watched out for everyone else's kids. There was always someone there if you needed them, and as I found out a time or two, there was also always someone ready to report anything I did wrong to my dad. With that many eyes on me, I quickly learned that I wasn't going to get away with much.

As we grew older, my parents realized that sharing a room with my little sister wasn't the best situation, and they moved me into the apartment next door with my Aunt Fanny, where I got to sleep on an extra bed they'd put in her bedroom. Fanny never married (we never knew why) and was not used to having kids around, so when I moved in, it was probably more of an adjustment for her than it was for me. Thankfully, though, she warmed up to me and even made sure I ate breakfast (usually oatmeal) every day before school.

Living so close to each other, we grew up understanding that family was very important. It was a given that all dinners would be with the family—there were no exceptions or excuses. On top of that, Sunday dinners were always at a restaurant, regardless of our financial state, and they were mandatory. Through these dinners and our family meals, we were exposed to different cuisines and ethnic dishes that included a rotation of seafood (Lundy Bros. in Sheepshead Bay, which only had African American waiters), Chinese, deli, and Italian food (Carolinas— which, to this day, had the best baked clams I've ever tasted).

With so much importance placed on food and family, it is somewhat ironic that a lack of food and family was the reason I taught myself how to cook. Let me explain: both of my parents worked, and like a lot of latchkey kids, there were times when I was left to fend for myself when it came to dinner. Around the age of 12, though, I grew tired of eating peanut butter and jelly sandwiches, so it was out of necessity that I taught myself how to cook. Initially, I started out small, fixing something that was easy to throw together, but as I got better at cooking, I dug into cookbooks to find more interesting and complex recipes, which I'd sometimes put my own touch on to make them even better. It wasn't long before I realized that cooking for myself wasn't a chore at all—it was actually therapeutic, and I found that I enjoyed it so much that I looked forward to cooking and experimenting in the kitchen. Fast forward to today, and I can cook just about anything … and often without a recipe. I can eat something in a restaurant and identify the flavors and ingredients and then recreate it at home. The first try is usually close, but the second attempt is spot on. On the third take, I'm usually tweaking the recipe in some way to improve or enhance the dish and make it my own. I enjoy it so much that cooking would be my full-time career if it paid the bills—but it doesn't. So, instead, I choose to cook because I want to, and it gives me pleasure to share the dishes I create with my family and friends.

Life on West 29th Street wasn't just about food and family, though. It wasn't Disneyland by any stretch of the imagination, but we managed to have fun. When I walked out our front door, I didn't have to look very far to find friends or something to do. The kids on 29th Street grew up playing in the street, literally playing games *in the street*—punchball, stick ball, you name it, we did it. It was dangerous, sure, and several kids on our block did get hit by cars over the years—thankfully, no one was seriously hurt. Kids today aren't allowed to play in the streets, but this was a different time—life was at a slower pace, and it was common for children to be unsupervised and have the freedom to explore and play in the street and anywhere else.

In my younger years, I knew I had to stay close to home, but as I grew older, those boundaries expanded. I was about ten years old when my friends and I were allowed to go to the beach without our parents. We lived right next to some old commercial buildings that were in the initial stages of being redeveloped. The buildings and auto repair shops were replaced with an A&P supermarket, which just so happened to be within walking distance of Gravesend Bay on one side and the Atlantic Ocean (and the beach) on the other. The surrounding neighborhood was a conglomeration of Jews (usually second generation from Europe) and Italian immigrants from the lower east side of Manhattan and African Americans. But as time went on, total neglect by city officials caused the neighborhood to fall from poor to worse. With each passing year, there was an increase of influx of folks from Puerto Rico, which changed the complexion of the neighborhood. This was a problem for some, but it didn't bother me at all. I was more interested in sports, and our youth teams were composed of a mix of ethnicities. Looking back, I'm grateful that I grew up in a mixed neighborhood, and I believe the experience shaped my desire to learn about other cultures and helped me feel comfortable in later years when I had the pleasure of visiting other countries. While they certainly aren't like the community I grew up in, I sometimes have to remind myself that New York City was a melting pot with a little bit of everything. Growing up in that melting pot taught me to respect different cultures and ethnicities, and it played a big role as I learned how to navigate Russia, China, and the rest of the world. And to think, this exposure got its start when I was playing sports with the kids in the neighborhood.

I credit my father with my love for sports. He actually grew up in the same neighborhood, where he had made a name and reputation for himself as an athlete. During summer, I spent Saturdays and Sundays watching him pitch in the local softball leagues, and in the winter, he played football in the park by our house on Sundays. Football was truly a neighborhood favorite, and all the adults played—some even played professional football—and when we were old enough, they let us kids join in. It wasn't the NFL, but I had the opportunity to play football with and against my dad, and I witnessed his passion and skill firsthand. He was good—and being big and strong as hell, he was built like a football player. As a matter of fact, my father dreamed of playing professional football, and I think he would have made it, but he tabled that dream to join the Army when the war broke out. When he came back to the States, he had been injured, but it was a sacrifice he was willing to make. Patriotic and passionate, he considered it his duty to fight for his country.

These were the influences I grew up with on West 29th Street. We didn't have everything, but we had everything we needed. At the time, we didn't know that we were poor or that we lived in a rough part of town. After all, we didn't have the Internet or social media, so we had nothing to compare ourselves to. When you don't know what you're missing, you don't miss it. But we did know that we were rich in other ways—we had a close family, food to eat, and friends to play with. It wasn't until years later that I was exposed to a different way of life. While my home life shaped my childhood, my education and entry into the working world actually shaped my life in unbelievable ways, transitioning me from Larry Namer, the least likely to … to Larry Namer, international media mogul.

CHAPTER 2 MAKING FRIENDS, NOT WAR

It is not possible for me to look back on my childhood without thinking of my friends. To this day, they are still my strongest and longest friendships. We went to Mark Twain Junior High School in Brooklyn together. Coming from Coney Island, it would have been surprising for any of us to make it to Hollywood, but oddly enough, three of us ended up having prominent positions in the entertainment industry. Besides me, there was Stan Rogow, who produced Lizzy Maguire for Disney, and Elliot Lurie, the most studious one in our group who went to Rutgers, even though his heart was always in music. Elliot formed a band called Looking Glass and wrote and sang the song, Brandy. Still popular and played widely, Brandy is considered to be one of the top 50 summer songs of all time. The song was revitalized in the film Master of the Universe 2, and one of the characters in the movie declared it to be the greatest song ever on earth. Elliot went on to become the head of music for Fox; now he tours solo, and, of course, Brandy is the most requested tune.

From Mark Twain, I went on to attend Stuyvesant High School in Manhattan, an all-boys school that was a 1.25-hour train ride from my home. At that time, junior high students had to test before being admitted to Stuyvesant, and less than one percent of the students who applied were accepted. This wasn't important to me because I had no interest in going there, but after the son of one of my dad's friends got in, my dad was determined that I go there, too. I wasn't a great student, but apparently, I was accepted because I had a high IQ and lots of potential. While Stuyvesant was considered prestigious, I hated it and begged to transfer to Abraham Lincoln High School, where most of my friends from Coney Island and surrounding neighborhoods went. It was also around that time that I discovered girls, so being stuck in an all-boys school didn't fit my social agenda.

I'll be the first to admit that I used to hate girls, at least until something changed my thinking in about the sixth grade. I had been invited to a birthday party for my cousin, Martin Namer. Initially, I didn't want to go, but my parents made me. It was there that we played party games—spin the bottle and seven minutes in heaven. In this case, heaven was a clothes closet, and I found myself there with Hilary, a girl who was a year older than me. So there I was in heaven with Hilary, and we kissed. My life was forever changed.

I didn't want to go to an all-boys school. To me, it wasn't a privilege to attend a prestigious school—no, it felt like a punishment. Every day, I was on the subway with fellow Mark Twain classmates Robert Ismach and Louis Handwerker—Louis was the nephew of Nathan Handwerker, the founder of Nathan's, the famous hot dog stand. I wasn't about to give in and kept on begging my parents until they finally relented, and in the middle of my sophomore year, I transferred to Lincoln.

Lincoln served three surrounding areas as the primary public high school. Let's just say they were poor, moderately poor, and a group we thought of as the rich kids, not because they were wealthy, but because they weren't as poor as the rest of us. Remarkably, more Nobel Prize winners have graduated from Lincoln than any other school in America.

And like Mark Twain, Lincoln could boast some big names in the entertainment industry, like Neil Diamond, Neil Sedaka, Lou Gossett, Jr., The Tokens, Harvey Keitel, Mel Brooks, and Buddy Rich. Nobody really knows why so many from Lincoln had such fame, but we jokingly say there must have been something in the water.

Like I said, it was during my junior and senior high school years that my greatest and longest lasting friendships were forged. My earliest best friend was Jimmy Doyle, an Irish American. In high school, my friend group was mainly from the football team, and I was closest to Al Smith (we called him Junior) and Frank Gibson, who were both African American. As a senior, I became very close with Andy Berdy and his family. Andy came from a military family; his dad was a colonel, and his brother, Mike, went to West Point. It was devastating when Mike died in Vietnam during Christmas, and it was devastating not just to Andy but to all around him. It was also very pivotal in my world and political perceptions.

I went to Mike's funeral in West Point and was surprised at how stoic everyone was. With a stiff upper lip, no one cried, and that seemed odd to me. While I tried to follow suit, I finally lost it during the rifle salute. This was during the Vietnam War, and I was pro war and frowned upon the protestors on college campuses. One day, Andy's dad and I were having a conversation, and he said something that opened my eyes. Suddenly, I could see what was going on beyond the rhetoric of saving us from communism. It was these conversations (which surprised me coming from Andy's dad) that made me rethink my ideas about our government, politicians, and Americas role in the world.

While Andy didn't make it through West Point, he did make the military his life, and his sons followed suit. Still friends, we have always been able to have civil discourse and discussions about controversial subjects, like politics, wars, and foreign policy. Because of Andy and his family, I learned to examine things carefully and rationally, instead of simply blindly accepting whatever I think or hear.

Coming from a poor area, most of the kids in our neighborhood didn't go to college, so they were drafted. I knew many of them. My cousin, Martin Namer, was shot down in his helicopter in Vietnam and died. Robert Alicia and several other members of our high school football team also died in Vietnam.

Eventually, I was drafted, too. Surprisingly, it was my father who did everything he could to prevent that from happening.

My dad was very patriotic, and he was proud to fight for his country, but my war hero dad was not going to see his son die in a war that was being fought for reasons he did not understand. This wasn't WWII, where my dad fought alongside fellow Americans for a *good cause*. No, this war was different—very different. My dad didn't buy into the government line on why we were there, and he even told me he would send me to Canada before he would let me get drafted to go to Vietnam. Instead, he took a second job working in a candy store so he could either pay for me to go for draft counselling or help me leave the country. While it was controversial, his insistence reflected just how strongly he felt about sending his son into a battle that he didn't believe in. When my cousin Martin was killed, his resolve to keep me out of the Army became even stronger.

I did go for counselling when I failed to maintain a passing average in community college. I got drafted and was called for a physical at Fort Hamilton on the same day as my friend, Ronnie Belgene, who also did not want to go and went through counselling. The day of our physical was something like a scene in a Woody Allen movie. And I had come prepared. As a kid, I'd had issues with my spine and had seen doctors about it. So I brought with me a letter from one of those doctors and the X-rays he had taken.

The night before the physical, Ronnie and I dropped mescaline (remember, this was the sixties), and we were still reeling when we got to our physical, along with hundreds of young guys who couldn't avoid the draft. They made us all strip naked, and, humiliated and vulnerable, we had to march through the physical exams. Thank goodness for the mescaline! They then proceeded to give us a form to fill out about our medical history, and I checked every box, stating I'd had just about every condition imaginable, as well as some that were beyond imagination altogether. From there, a doctor questioned me about all the illnesses I claimed to have had.

"I see you checked off that you have had a heart attack. Where were you hospitalized and when?"

I responded that I was too poor to go to a hospital, so I just stayed home and nursed myself back to good health.

"Ah, now I see you have had cancer. Tell me about that."

I told him I smoked cigarettes, and it says on the pack that smoking can cause lung cancer. The government wouldn't lie to me about that, would they?

When he asked where and when I was treated, I told him I couldn't afford to get treatment for lung cancer, either. For the second time, he shot me a disbelieving look.

He then continued down my checklist: Tuberculosis, bed wetting, wanting to kill my mother, having suicidal thoughts—you name it. I left no stone unturned. I even figured out how to fail the hearing test and was deemed to be deaf in my right ear. I also proclaimed to be a homosexual, even though I never acted on it.

Finally, the doctor made an observation. "I see you really want to be a Marine, right?"

To which I responded, "Yes, yes, give me a gun and let me kill."

He wrote on my forms "must see psychiatrist." But when I asked to see one, I was told, "Sorry, no one is available. Keep moving."

With the X-rays and letter about my back in hand, I asked to see the specialist and was told they were not seeing anyone that day. It was obvious that they were herding us off to war, no excuses allowed. So I took matters into my own hands and found out where the specialist office was and armed with my letter and x-rays, I walked naked across the base to his office. The assistant called him to the front, and when he saw me standing there in my birthday suit, he laughed. However, he did look at the letter and the X-rays. He stated he knew the doctor from medical school and that he was well respected. After writing on my forms, he told me to go back to the first building and see a processing officer.

When I looked at the forms, I noticed that he'd crossed off the comment about me seeing a psychiatrist, but I still didn't understand what was happening—that is, until the processing officer reviewed my forms, stamped some of my papers, and said, "Go home, soldier. You are not fit for duty."

I was 4-F.

I'll never forget the look on my dad's face when I told him I was out … or the fact that he handed me $50 and told me to go out and celebrate. Fifty dollars back then was more like $500 is today. I bought some hash and celebrated with my friends.

3 THE PATH LEAST LIKELY

Even though I didn't serve in the Vietnam War, it changed my life and my outlook. Having grown up in a patriotic family with a father who proudly served, I loved America and believed in the American dream. It just wasn't in me to conceive that our politicians or government could possibly be corrupt or do anything that wouldn't be in our best interests. The Vietnam War changed all that.

At the time, I was conservative; some might rightfully label me as preppy. As a kid, I played organized baseball, and in high school, I played football—great American sports. Off the field, I sported a crew cut and wore penny loafers, chino pants, and stadium jackets with toggle buttons. Quite the opposite of the hippies who protested against the war, I was appalled that they would dare to question our government and not support our troops. But when Andy Berdy's brother, Michael, was killed in combat, I gained a new perspective.

I remember sitting on Andy's porch in Seagate Brooklyn and telling his dad, who was an Army colonel, that the hippies needed to be beaten up. To my surprise, Colonel Berdy was very much against that and explained that Michael died in order for all Americans to be able to speak their mind and have dissenting positions. Even more, he didn't defend our role in the war, actually saying that we always have to question those who govern us. Outside of my father's desire to keep me out of the controversial war, it was the first time that I'd actually heard anything negative about Vietnam from a patriotic military veteran.

After that, my cousin, Marty, was killed in Vietnam, as well as several other guys I knew from our neighborhood and my high school football team. Now that the effects were hitting close to home, I started to wake up and, like Colonel Berdy advised, question the government and our role in Nam. That's when I did what was previously unthinkable—I stopped cutting my hair, traded my chinos for bell bottoms, and officially became a hippy.

Let me tell you, if there was ever a time to be a hippy, it was in the late 60s. If there was ever a place to be a hippy, it was Woodstock.

It was 1969, and my high school friend, Phil Sloves, and I both attended Brooklyn College when we decided to go to Woodstock with Phil's younger brother, Tyler. At the time, my high school sweetheart, Nancy Stein, happened to have a cousin who rented a summer cabin a few miles from the concert site in upstate New York, and we took advantage of the opportunity to stay there. By then, I fit in with the massive crowd and was a full-fledged hippy, long hair, beard, and hippy garb all the way. Interestingly, though, while drugs were the rage at the time, I didn't really like pot and rarely smoked it, even at Woodstock, where everyone was passing around a pipe or a joint and getting high.

Not me, though. I was there because just about all of my favorite bands and artists were there, and I didn't want to miss what would be the concert of a lifetime. I got to see the Who's Who of 60's rock and roll.

And it didn't disappoint. Woodstock left a lifelong impression on me, so much so that in later years when I was doing concerts in Russia, I would invite all the folks that fascinated me during that time with the hopes of talking to them and maybe even having a drink together. One of my favorite memories was getting shit-faced drunk with Joe Cocker at the Europa Hotel in Saint Petersburg. The only thing that would have been better was if Joplin and Hendrix had still been alive.

Fun was fun, and while I partook in it whenever I could, I was still in college, and I still needed to work. Back in the day, being a student wasn't a full-time "job." I still had to pay my way. So I did what I'd done since I was 12 years old helping my dad on his Pepsi truck—I worked. Since that time, I've racked up quite a resume. I sold cigarettes at Cheap Joe's Discount Store in Coney Island and served as a counselor at YMCA Day Camp and a basketball coach at the Flatbush Boys Club. I was also a delivery driver for House of King Chinese restaurant in Brooklyn, which was where I learned to cook Chinese food, and I was a cook at a pizza place on Wall Street. At one time, I delivered cars for a body shop in Brooklyn, and I was even a taxi driver in New York City—that is, until I got robbed at gunpoint … the second time. I even sold bananas in Harlem for my dad's brother, Al the Banana King, and had a gig selling tickets to the Magic Carpet Ride at Coney Island's amusement park.

They were all jobs … but they weren't careers. I never wanted to be a delivery driver, and I certainly didn't want to be a three-time victim of robbery in a New York City cab. Being the first in our family to earn a college degree, I graduated from Brooklyn College with a degree in economics and the dream of getting my first full-time job as a teacher. That's right—I wanted to stand at the front of a classroom and make a difference by imparting my wisdom on eager young minds.

I'll never know if that would have worked out, because with one swift action, New York changed my career … and the trajectory of my life.

It was in the early 70s, and New York found itself in a severe budget crisis that caused them to place a five-year moratorium on hiring teachers. Devastated, I had no choice but to look for employment elsewhere. At the time, my girlfriend Nancy's father, who was in the electrician's union, introduced me to a new field that was just emerging—cable television. He said he doubted anyone would ever pay for TV, but since this was going to be a temporary job, why not do it? Thinking it would be temporary, a way to earn money until I could figure out another way to use my degree, I applied for a job.

I didn't have any qualms about being underqualified for the job. On the contrary, as a college graduate, I believed I was overqualified. It was a blue-collar job, and I thought they wouldn't hire me if they knew I had a degree because they'd (rightfully) assume I was biding my time until I could get a better job. So I left out that little detail about having a college degree when I applied. Not too long after, they found me out.

Who would have thought that biding my time turned into a 50-year career that changed the trajectory of my career and my life?

Like most people in 1971, I had no idea what cable television was when I was hired as an assistant underground splicer for Manhattan Cable. That's right—I wasn't even a splicer—I was an *assistant* splicer, underground, at that, which was about as low as you could get on the totem pole. But it was $90 a week, and I could learn the tricks of the trade rather quickly.

While I had no idea what cable television really was, I quickly learned that my job was a "dirty" job, much like the jobs Mike Rowe featured on his TV show, "Dirty Jobs." Each day, I'd take the subway into the city, open the manhole covers, crawl into the sewers, and report for work. I worked in the underbelly of New York City's streets, where I helped splice the cables together, next to the rats and roaches that scurried about. It was dark and damp and the work was tough, but I quickly adapted, learning how to handle the technical equipment with surprising ease. My ability to catch on quickly got noticed, and it wasn't long before I moved up from being an assistant to a full-fledged splicer, and then to a construction worker who climbed through Manhattan's backyards to pull wires.

I worked in a division run by Frank Chiaino, who, despite his lack of fancy degrees, became the Vice President of Operations. Frank "discovered" me and was responsible for elevating me through the ranks. He also taught me how to motivate people and get the most out of them.

It was during this time at Manhattan Cable that I met someone who was very influential in my career. Nick Nicholas was sent in by Time Inc. (now our owner) to take the reins as president of MC TV. He was a mentor who instilled in me the principle of being "firm but fair," emphasizing that effective leadership is built on a foundation of integrity and fairness. This principle became the cornerstone of my management style.

When I met Nick, I was a member of the union. My role in the union provided me with a unique perspective on the dynamics between management and workers. It allowed me to see both sides of the equation and understand the importance of clear communication and mutual respect. Nick taught me that while it was important to be firm in my decisions, it was equally crucial to be fair in how I treated people. Whether I was dealing with employees, negotiating with vendors, or managing projects, I always aimed to ensure that everyone felt respected and treated fairly, even if they didn't always agree with my decisions. This approach not only helped me build strong, trusting relationships but also established my reputation as a fair and reliable leader. His advice was invaluable as I moved up the ranks, helping me to navigate the complexities of leadership with empathy and fairness.

"The Negotiator"

My technical proficiency and ability to bridge the gap between workers and management didn't go unnoticed, and I was asked to join the negotiating committee for the union. My success in that endeavor led to an unexpected opportunity when I was appointed as the Vice Chairman of the Cable TV Workers Division of the Electrical Workers Union at the age of 23. It was a far cry from being a teacher, but it put me in a unique position of influence and responsibility at a very young age. Sitting at the negotiation table, I served as a translator between the company executive and the ground-floor union workers. As I applied everything Nick had taught me in these transactions, my goal was to make sure both sides felt heard and respected. It was then that I was nicknamed "The Negotiator."

Ironically, my ability to negotiate on behalf of others created another opportunity. This time, however, the deal I was negotiating was my own. When I was offered a position in management, I initially resisted. When I finally relented and accepted the offer, I jokingly said that "I had been sold into slavery."

Little did I know, but I had been given the opportunity of a lifetime, and everything I had done up to that point had put me in the right place at the right time for that role. More than anything, though, this young man who had grown up in poverty in Coney Island and hadn't been able to use his college degree for one single day, and who got his start making $90 a week working underground with rats, learned one invaluable lesson:

"If I can do it, so can you."

4 FINDING OPPORTUNITY IN ADVERSITY

Despite my initial reluctance to join the management ranks, I somehow managed to adapt quite well to the change, though I have to admit it was quite a shift. I went from being on the ground, literally working in the trenches, to making decisions that impacted the entire company and all of its employees. Having never been in a position like this before, I learned very quickly that this new role demanded an entirely different set of skills and a much broader perspective than anything I'd done in the past, and if I was going to be successful, I knew I had to learn quickly and figure out how to adapt to the challenges of leading a large team.

Thankfully, I already had one ability that would be key to my success: the ability to simplify complex problems. Even when I had been splicing and pulling wires, I always took the time to figure out what I was doing and why. In order to do the job right, I did something that I later learned others skipped over—I read whatever manual or instructions I was given. Then I took it one step further, and I followed directions meticulously. Unbeknownst to me at the time, this led to my ability to find innovative solutions. It also surprised a few people, who would ask me how I knew so much so quickly.

My response, "I read the manual."

It seems that I was the exception, not the norm. Who knew that such a simple step would be such a novel concept?

During this time, I also relied heavily on the principle of being firm but fair, maintaining integrity, and ensuring that everyone felt respected and valued. I have both Frank and Nick to thank for instilling those principles into me early on. They definitely knew what they were talking about, because I can attest that they were crucial to my leadership success. These principles not only helped me earn the trust of my team, but they also helped me navigate some unchartered territories, like corporate politics, which was extremely foreign to me at the time.

It was these principles and my straightforward approach that led to my rapid ascent within Manhattan Cable, where I was appointed Director of Operations at the young age of 25. This role was both a significant achievement and a substantial challenge. I was responsible for managing over 300 employees and overseeing all aspects of the company's operations, except for programming and finance. Again, I found that I had a lot to learn, but as it had been in the past, my deep understanding of both the technical and human elements of the business enabled me to excel in this role.

I found myself on the ground floor of innovation in an industry that was in its infancy. Everything and anything we implemented had the potential to be innovative and groundbreaking, which was actually quite incredible. Think about it—with cable TV being so young, the possibilities were limited only by our imaginations. It was an exciting time, as we coupled that innovation with the business practices that led to profits, development, and the growth that made cable a household name.

And I was fortunate to be at the forefront of it all.

My final role at Manhattan Cable was as the Director of Corporate Development, a position that allowed me to fully explore my innovative and visionary side. I felt like I'd come full circle, starting from the ground up (actually below ground) and moving up the ranks. I knew everything there was to know about cable television as it existed, but in this new role, I was responsible for the future of cable. Charged with finding new uses for cable television other than good reception or entertainment, I spearheaded projects that were ahead of their time and set the stage for future advancements in the industry.

One of the pioneering projects I led involved remote medical diagnostics, a concept that was revolutionary in the early days of cable technology. We envisioned a system where doctors could consult with patients remotely, using the cable network to transmit medical data from one building or office to another. It was a concept that was ahead of its time, showcasing the potential of cable television beyond mere entertainment.

Limited only by our imaginations, it was exciting to envision new, innovative ways to incorporate technology across multiple industries. From medicine, we tapped into financial institutions and developed a system for data transmission between banks. This project highlighted the versatility of cable technology and its potential to revolutionize various industries by providing secure and efficient communication channels. These initiatives not only demonstrated the breadth of possibilities within the cable industry but also positioned Manhattan Cable as a leader in technological innovation. Beyond those mentioned, we pioneered security systems, computer information systems, and a bunch of other things. Remember, this was before anyone even dreamed of the Internet.

In my role, I was fortunate to participate in numerous think tanks and conferences focused on the future relationship between people and technology. These gatherings were instrumental in shaping my vision and solidifying my reputation as a forward-thinking leader in the field. They provided a platform to exchange ideas with other innovators and stay ahead of emerging trends and technologies.

All in all, the decade I spent working for Manhattan Cable was invaluable in shaping my career. The relationships I gained during those years were formative in my growth and leadership style. Yet, every step was a learning process that instilled in me the basic principles of success in an industry that thrived on being on the cutting edge of innovation. It was an exciting time in a constantly evolving industry, and I'm not sure which one of us grew fastest—Larry Namer or cable television.

Regardless how one might answer that, I like to think that my time at Manhattan Cable influenced the cable television industry long after I moved on. I know that my time spent there continued to influence my career over the decades, and I will forever be grateful for the education, relationships, experiences, and opportunities that Manhattan Cable brought to my life.

I'm especially thankful that New York had placed a moratorium on hiring teachers—proof that anyone can find opportunity in adversity. I've said it before, and I'll say it again, "If I could do it, so can you."

5 LA, LIBERACE, AND ME

My last gig at Manhattan Cable was as the Director of Corporate Development, where I was charged with finding new uses for cable television, at a time when the industry was known for providing programming and good reception. I was at the ripe old age of 30 and was one of the only people who knew how to build an underground cable system. It was the early 1980s, and you could say that cable was in its dinosaur and pre-Internet stages. I was just getting a glimpse into what was possible. We were doing remote medical diagnostics, stock quotation services, and moving data between banks, the downtown, on Wall Street, Uptown, and Eastside. At the time, these endeavors were quite advanced—fax machines hadn't even been born, so we were, indeed, just breaking the surface of what cable television could someday be.

As I envisioned potential ideas and uses for cable, I had to think ahead of my time. What kind of relationship will people have with technology in the year 2000? While we were just delving into bit and bytes, big cities were joining in, realizing that they, too, wanted cable—and like Manhattan, they also wanted to go underground.

At that time, there was a company from Canada that won the franchise for a big piece of Los Angeles in the San Fernando Valley. Like the other cities climbing abord the cable train, they were looking for someone to come in and build this underground cable system. And because I was the only with that experience, they turned to me.

There was one problem—I wasn't interested. And even though they were persistent, I refused their job offer, several times, in fact. No way was this New York kid going to Hollywood. La La Land was the polar opposite of Coney Island, and I didn't want any part of it.

And I did everything in my power to make it seemingly impossible for them to recruit me.

The executive recruiter was none other than the son of Sugar Ray Robinson—that's right—the son of the famed boxer who by then had earned celebrity status. Still, I wasn't interested. After a few flat-out refusals, the chairman of the Canadian company called me in an attempt to persuade me to change my mind.

"I'm only asking you to come out so I can talk to you," he said.

"I told you I'm not interested."

"Okay, here's what I can do. I'll fly you out with the girlfriend and put you in the Bel Aire Hotel. I just want an hour of your time."

Seeing that he wasn't going to give up easily, I thought, *What the hell? If he's paying for it, I'll go see what he has to say, but it's not going to do him any good. I'm not taking the job.*

And I told him so.

"As long as you understand there's no way I'm taking the job, I'll fly out and give you an hour of my time," I replied.

When I got there, I was a total dickhead. Rude and unapproachable, I sat down and said, "Okay, your hour starts right now. Go ahead, tell me what you've got."

He looked at me and came right and asked me for the bottom line.

"What would it take for you to move out here, Larry?"

I don't think he was ready for my demands, because I made them so unbelievable that nobody in their right mind would be able to meet them.

"I want four times what I make in New York. And I understand Liberace doesn't live in LA anymore. I think I'd like to live in a house with a piano-shaped swimming pool, if you know what I mean. And, hey, I want my own mobile phone and a company car, too."

I knew what I was asking for was outlandish, especially since there was no such thing as a cell phone back then. Naturally, he knew it, too.

"What you're asking for is nuts," he commented.

"Exactly," I responded. "I told you I don't want this job."

We got a good laugh out of that, and I left, thinking that was that. I'd finally laid their offer to rest.

I was surprised when he called me with another offer, which was twice what I was making in New York. Still, I didn't budge.

"You don't understand, I wasn't negotiating with you. You asked me what it would take. I told you what it would take, and that's it."

Figuring my refusal probably spooked him, I hung up the phone, but it wasn't long before I wondered if I had made a mistake—I mean, his offer really was a good one.

Our back-and-forth negotiations took place in the middle of the winter, and I was in New York. Every morning, I'd put my suit on and go to work, ready to start my day. If you've ever been to New York, you know it's beautiful when it snows—for a day. But fast forward to the next day and that blanket of glistening white snow had all turned to soot, and I stepped out to the curb right when a truck drove by and splashed cold black snow and water all over my freshly cleaned suit.

Oh God, are you kidding me? What the hell am I doing here? I thought as I looked at my suit in disgust.

When I walked into my office, my assistant informed me that "that guy" had called me again. His timing must've been right because I said, "Alright. Get him on the phone."

The last time I'd talked to him, he had thought my demands were absurd, but this time, I was the one who was surprised.

"What you asked for is ridiculous, but we will do it. When can you be here?"

All it took was one glance at how wet and dirty I was, and I knew my answer.

"How about two weeks?" I responded.

That was the end of my Manhattan cable years—ten years that took me from the underbelly of the streets of New York to the top of the corporate ladder.

True to their word, they did put me in Liberace's old house, and I was fascinated with it, swimming pool and all. There I was, a Brooklyn kid who hilariously dared to ask to live in a house that I'd only seen on TV, knowing in my mind that there was absolutely no way they'd ever agree to that. But they did. They rented the house, and that's where I lived. I have to admit it was pretty cool when my friends from Brooklyn came out to visit. After all, this house was featured in the opening of Entertainment Tonight every evening. When I told my mother, she thought I was on drugs and there was no way I would be living in this famous house. Sometimes it didn't feel possible that I would be living that kind of life. I literally went from 14th Street in Manhattan and threw my stuff into a truck and moved to the land of the stars.

This 30-year-old from Manhattan Cable was now working as the General Manager and Vice President for Cable America (a subsidiary of Cable Casting Limited of Canada) in Los Angeles. All of the operating departments reported to me, and I was also responsible for the finance, marketing, and programming. To top it off, we did have 61 channels to work with, but at the time, there weren't 61 channels in existence, so we had to invent the channels to fill those slots. And that is exactly what we did.

We hit the ground running and were only limited by our imaginations. It was actually fun to do things no one had ever thought of before. We had town hall meetings and talked to politicians and polled the public to see what they wanted. In the end, *Forbes* magazine named our company to be the national model for cable programming, with one of our first new technologies being the introduction of Pay per View, where people could watch a movie at home at the same time it was released in the theaters.

The first one was actually the movie about The Doors. Some of the members of the Doors came to the studio, like Robbie Krieger—Jim Morrison was already dead—and we made it happen. It was actually rather inexpensive to do, but it showed me that people would be willing to do it if we made it interesting enough and added value. Now, we had to make sure that the experience we created was different than going to the movies. We had to talk to some of the guys that were in the movie and bring them into people's living rooms to make it special and something they'd be willing to pay for.

And as soon as we gave them a taste of what cable television could really be, the sky was the limit. We had 61 channels to fill … and I knew we could do it.

6 AN INSTANT, THREE AND A HALF YEAR SUCCESS

The years I spent creating Valley Cable were filled with challenges and opportunities. First, I was charged with supervising departments I had no experience with, and my role within the company was on a far larger scale than the one I'd held at Manhattan Cable. Top that with the fact that I was in Los Angeles, where the atmosphere and lifestyle was unlike anything I'd ever known in Coney Island, and it's safe to say I was out of my comfort zone.

If anyone had said I had a lot to learn, they wouldn't be wrong.

If they said that I wouldn't let that stand in my way, they'd be right.

The truth was, I was just naïve enough to believe that I was up for the job … and confident enough that I didn't let my lack of experience stand in my way. Sure, I was young and knew nothing about celebrities and the entertainment world, but I didn't care. This 31-year-old former cable splicer from the ghetto was up for the challenge.

Outside of creating the different departments, my main mission was to fill 61 channels with content that people would want to watch—

something that had never been done before. At that time, there were a handful of major networks, but few other options for television viewers in LA … or anywhere, for that matter. Coming up with affordable ideas for shows that would appeal to the public was quite the task, and we were open to anything—dedicating one channel to featuring lost and found pets says it all. But we had plenty of channels to fill, and we knew we had to get creative to do it.

In just three years, we successfully built the first 61-channel 2-way interactive cable system in the United States. And we did it so well that Forbes magazine gave us an award, declaring that Valley was the national model for cable programming. To think that it all started with just two pieces of paper, which they literally handed me when I got off the plane in LA. One was the franchise that the city gave to them, stating what I had to build. The other was the credit line from Toronto Dominion Bank telling me what I had to do to draw the money I needed to build it.

Frankly, I had so much freedom that I felt like a kid in a candy store. With 61 channels to create, we played with a lot of programming ideas and had the liberty to try a lot of unusual things. On a low budget, being in the heart of Hollywood helped. We had access to a lot of famous people and celebrities, and I was fortunate to work with some innovative people who helped fill those channels with the school library channel, the school lunch channel, the city government channel, and the lost pets channel.

We also created a production team that won awards for new shows, such as the Rascado and Dos, which is Spanish for "one heart broken in two"—a new show dedicated to LA's Mexican population that represented being torn between two countries and two cultures. That and other shows won us an Ace Award, which is the cable version of an Emmy, and a feather we proudly wore on our programming hat.

Our success sparked my interest in understanding how far our programming opportunities could really go. In Manhattan, I'd been responsible for identifying non-entertainment uses for cable, but I was now on the other side of the business, discovering how to use cable television in a way that would open up the entertainment world in new and exciting ways.

That's why I chose to build and lead one of the most advanced cable systems in the world. One of the most memorable projects I led was the implementation of a new, more efficient service system. This involved not only optimizing our operations but also innovating in ways that had never been done before in the industry. For example, we developed a 61-channel two-way interactive cable system, the first of its kind, which became a national model for cable programming and earned recognition from *Forbes Magazine.*

When Valley announced that they were selling the company and going back to Canada, I had the opportunity to go with them. But I declined. I wasn't about to go from New York to Los Angeles, only to end up in Toronto. The climate was one reason I'd moved to LA, and I'd grown quite accustomed to it. Canada just wasn't on my radar.

It was then that Alan Mruvka and I started playing around with the idea of forming our own company. Alan, while having a degree in architecture, was as interested as I was in delving deeper into the world of entertainment. So in 1984, we created the business plan for the Movietime Channel, Inc., which later was narrowed down to Movietime before we realized that we didn't want to limit ourselves solely to movies, so we renamed it "E!" to encompass all avenues of entertainment.

It simply made sense. When you're in Rome, do as the Romans do, right? Well, Los Angeles is one of the few cities that is totally dominated by a single industry. Much like Detroit is the automotive center, LA is the entertainment capital of the country, if not the entire world. Entertainment is its entire culture.

After moving to LA and being in the heart of the entertainment world, I would see my neighbors and friends going to prestigious movie premieres and parties, and like most people, I wanted to be a part of that world, as well. So I picked up the phone and called the studios, asking to be put on the list. After all, I was known for creating the cable company that aired the shows and the stars. But the response I got wasn't what I was looking for.

"Larry, you are running a cable construction company. You know we won't put you on our guest list."

It was like being told I represented the phone company or the gas company. They wouldn't put me on a list because they saw me as a utility company, rather than a media conglomerate.

Not one to give up easily, I pushed a bit farther, but the answer didn't change. They were adamant that they weren't going to put me on a premiere list.

I'd been innovative before, so I put on my thinking cap and came up with an idea. I called back and said, "Listen, the most effective marketing vehicle that you have for the movies is the movie trailer."

(I made sure I repeated that more than a few times.)

"Now, we both know that little two-minute trailer is often better than the movie itself. And we know that you use the best two minutes to promote a 50-million-dollar movie! Tell me something: why do I only see movie trailers when I'm already in the movie theater? Don't you think that you should be showing these to people when they're home and make them want to go to the movies?"

While they argued that they couldn't do that because airtime was expensive, I knew I was onto something. I had my opening and took it. Thanks to Valley Cable, my access to celebrities was just a channel away.

"Okay," I said, "I'll tell you what. I have a channel that I'll put your movie trailers on, but you have to put me on the party and premiere lists."

Bingo! I found my ticket, and they agreed to put me on the list to attend their premieres, as long as I put the movie channels on our dedicated channel, aptly called The Trailer Channel.

To their surprise, surveys showed that The Trailer Channel was an audience favorite. They went from loving ESPN and MTV, channels that cost a hundred million dollars, to loving our trailer channel, which cost nothing. Not only did it give us access to the stars, but it gave us an opportunity when we formed E!.

It was Alan who had the idea. Alan was my friend from New Jersey, and he and I partnered together when Valley sold the company. It was Alan who said he wanted to create a channel like MTV, but for the movies. It was an interesting concept, especially since I had so much success with the trailer channel. There's really no difference between standing a host in front of a green screen who points at the screen and announces, "Madonna has a new music video," than having a host—a movie jock, if you will—stand in front of the same screen, announcing, "Schwarzenegger has a new movie."

It was like a light bulb went off! There was no need to recreate the wheel; we just had to figure out different ways to use it! Movies, TV, and all other forms of entertainment other than music were not given in-depth coverage. Studios would fight to get 20 seconds on Entertainment Tonight.

So we sat down and wrote a business plan, certain that it was such a good idea that somebody would love it and give us the funding to get started.

Being from Coney Island, I was tough and didn't give up easily, but even I didn't think it would take as long as it did to find someone to fund us. How long did it take? Three years—three and a half years to be exact—and even then, it was a tough sell.

We heard all the excuses—it's a nice idea, but if it's so great, how come somebody hasn't already done it? If it's such a good idea, Robert Murdoch would already be doing it. Then there was the "regular people don't start TV networks, only big media companies do that. You're not Warner Brothers, Time Incorporated, or Fox; you can't compete with those folks."

Then, we finally met a guy in New York who said he wanted to give us money. Jeff Pollack was heading the investment banking arm of Mavon Nuggent, a traditional Wall Street bond house. This was the break we needed.

"You know, the range for starting a network is 60 to 100 million," I said. "Could you make it closer to 100 so we can do all the things we have planned?"

He knocked us down with his reply, "Oh, no, I'm only allowed to sign for two and a half."

With the low end being 60 million, we asked him what the hell we were going to do with two and a half. They didn't budge and said that was all they could do, but they could help raise some more. With that, Alan and I looked at each other. Knowing we didn't have any other offers on the table, we decided to take the two and a half and figure out the rest.

At the time, I had a friend named Brian Owens, who was teaching radio, television, and film at the University of Texas in Austin. We went back to the days when I worked at Valley Cable. I gave him a call and told him about our idea. When he said he loved the idea, I mentioned that he probably had students who would likely relish Hollywood internships. That call landed us 31 kids from UT Texas in Austin who spent the summer getting us off the ground. Once we launched—in record time of three months from funding—many of these interns loved being with us so much, they stayed in LA. Most people don't realize, thinking of E! today, that it started with 11 employees and 31 interns. We brought in some really great people from the local cable scene who were experts on how to stretch a dollar. Brian Owens came back from Texas. Rick Portin from Viacom, San Francisco, came to be head of production. And Phil Quepschke and Mark Hale came from Falcon Cable.

With a staff in place, we turned our attention to getting the equipment we needed. With such a low budget to work with, we couldn't buy broadcast-level equipment, so we went to auctions and found equipment corporations had used for training films. It was a step above garage sale finds, but keep in mind that we were more than 95 million short of what a major production company would spend.

That meant we also didn't have money for fancy graphics, but we managed to find a graphic system that was used by the Air Force to train pilots and figured out how to use it for our purpose.

Somehow, we managed to make it work. It wasn't easy or fancy, but a lack of funding took that out of our control. The only thing we did have control over was selecting our hosts, so we opted to put the majority of the money we did have into that search. After all, the hosts would be the face of our channel and the representatives of our brand.

When all was said and done, there were those who said we were lucky in finding our hosts, but I beg to differ—there was no luck involved at all. Our search was very deliberate, it took thousands of taped interviews to find our first five hosts. It was hardly a small task, but it was well worth it with the hosts who ultimately joined us: the Academy Award-winning Greg Kinnear; Julie Moran, who went on to be the first woman to do Wide World of Sports; Katie Wagner, who later hosted "Lifestyles of the Rich and Famous;" Mark DeCarlo, who you might know from "Studs;" Chris Chisholm; and Suzanne Kay. They are all talented, and they all went on to make big names for themselves.

In the end, we were an instant, three and a half year, success. I give those kids a lot of the credit. They started as interns, and by the end of the summer, half of them were our vice presidents. That's how quickly we took off and grew.

When we went on the air at the end of July in that same year, all of those people who shot us down when we asked for money changed their tune, saying, "That's what you wanted to do? We would have given you the money three years ago if we knew that was what you were doing!"

We grew so quickly that in the first year, we were in 14 different countries, proving what we'd known all along—that it wasn't just people in America who loved Hollywood. People around the world loved celebrities, movies, and the gossip that came with them. Our concept had the international appeal that enabled us to do what everyone else said was impossible. A couple of regular guys from New York proved that they could, in fact, create a media company that not only could compete with Murdoch and Time, but could outcompete them.

But the fun was just getting started. Alan and I had big ideas and plans for E!

We wanted to change the entertainment industry … and in doing so, we ended up changing people's lives the Hollywood way—by making them stars. Movietime (later E!) made the wise decision to headquarter in Hollywood. While Hollywood was seen internationally as the center of the film and entertainment industry, oddly there was not a single TV network based there. We were now Hollywood's own channel and were quickly embraced by studios, celebrities, and local politicians.

CHAPTER 7

E! AND THE CHANNEL THAT NEVER WAS

Hollywood is funny stuff, and I'm not talking about comedy. Hollywood is strange. Alan and I knew better than to make believe it was rocket science, so we approached it very whimsically. For that reason, we envisioned that our channel would celebrate the industry, rather than focusing on what everyone else wanted to do, which was to blast evil gossip and destroy marriages and lives. We wanted to celebrate the uniqueness that is Hollywood and the people in it—the actors, actresses, and filmmakers. Ironically, we were able to "authentically" do so because we were a low-budget channel, not despite of that fact.

The truth of the matter was that not only did we buy used equipment, but that equipment also wasn't up to Hollywood's high standards. It was just a step above using home video equipment, meaning that the end result looked very pirate. People who watch actually commented that they felt like they were getting a personal glimpse into something they were not supposed to see. It was a far cry from what they were used to watching, and to our surprise, it was our ticket to integrate our whimsical approach, making it not only acceptable, but preferable, to create content without expensive equipment or fancy effects.

The biggest compliment was, "I feel like I'm a fly on the wall."

Bingo! That was exactly how we wanted our viewers to feel—as if they were eavesdropping on their favorite celebrities' personal lives and had an inside world into the lifestyles of the rich and very famous. The equipment just so happened to give it the authenticity to accomplish that task. It worked for us, so we had fun with it.

In the beginning, we didn't get any recognition. When we applied for press passes to get into the Academy Awards, we were rejected, saying something along the lines of "you're just a rinky dink little cable channel. The cable channel wouldn't even get us in, so we did what any reputable entertainment channel would do: we snuck into the Academy Awards that year. That's right—we literally jumped the fence!

Once inside, we wandered around, but unlike the other reporters and TV hosts, we didn't bother asking the stars about their next projects. There was no, "Tom Cruise, what can we look forward to next?" Instead, we took a different approach. "Hey, those clothes are really cool. Where did you get them?"

It was fun. It was positive. It was different. And to our surprise, it was so we received that it led to red carpets and filming the Hollywood jet set in their designer label outfits. The television audience loved it, and as a result, we started growing and getting more money. It wasn't long before the same cable companies that told us to go to hell when we asked for a press pass had to admit that what we were doing helped them promote their stars and movies. Suddenly, not only were they interested in giving us money, but they really wanted us to take it. (More on our search for partners and funding in the next chapter.)

The rest is history.

Let me drop a few names here. There's a good chance you've heard of some of the people who became famous (or more famous) because of E! Greg Kinnear and Ryan Seacrest are two. The list goes on to include Chelsea Handler, Kendra Wilkinson, Gulliana Rancic, Brooke Burke, Jules Asner, Cindy Taylor, John Henson, Joel McHale, and Hal Sparks, to name but a few. And I don't think it would be possible to talk about E! without mentioning the Kardashians—Kim, Khloe, and Kourtney— and their mom, Kris Jenner, and her husband, Bruce Jenner, who was one of the greatest Olympic athletes in the 1980s. Bruce and Kris were doing informercials before joining E! in 2007 when their show "Keeping Up With the Kardashians" launched and became a hit, proving that people wanted to know more about how celebrities lived their lives— they wanted to be a fly on the wall and see their homes and listen to their conversations.

It was right about that time that Alan and I were toying around the idea of starting another company, but this time, it would be focused on fitness and exercise. We'd call it FXTV, fitness and exercise television. It was simple, memorable, and we thought it was brilliant.

We had the logo and wrote the business plan, and to back it up, we formed a group of advisors that included renowned athletes like Kareem Abdul-Jabbar, OJ Simpson, and, of course, the Jenners. Believing we'd made a great channel, we started our money pitches to fund FXTV.

One of the places we pitched it to was the Fox Channel. At the time, Strauss Zelnick was the head of Fox, and when we talked to them, they liked the idea, but said they had plans to do something different. He was cordial about it, even thanking us for approaching them in a nice little letter he wrote to us, saying it was great to see us and that we had a good idea with our FXTV channel, but we're going in a different direction. They even invited us to call on them again if we came up with anything new.

It was all good … until we were reading one of the Hollywood industry trade publications and found out differently. Fox was announcing their new channel: FXTV—nothing to do with fitness and exercise, but they liked the name.

To say we were stunned would be an understatement. How could that be? After all, we owned the name and even registered it. It was legally ours, and we'd pitched it to enough people that that wasn't a secret. By this time, Zelnick was out, but we knew the folks at Fox—we were all friends and had promoted their shows and celebrities on E!—so we gave them a friendly phone call to find out what was going on. I'm not sure what happened, but their legal department, well, let's just say they weren't all that friendly. They came into the conversation with barrels loaded, saying that we should have never been granted the name FX, because all you had to do was put an O between the F and X, and it would spell Fox.

Like I said, we were among friends, but they were being such difficult idiots that they forced our hand. Little did they know at the time that we were already convinced that the channel didn't make sense. After all, we were still in the days of linear television. Logistically, it didn't work. If someone was just beginning yoga, they would want programming at that level, and as they practiced yoga, they'd advance, wanting programming at a higher level. So, when Fox pulled the name-grabbing stunt, we were already debating whether or not the FX channel was as good an idea as we originally thought. To top it off, we weren't really wed to the name—it was an idea, and we did the right thing by registering it so we had the legal right to use it, should we want to.

Our kid gloves came off when they told us that they were going to make sure we could never use the name that was legally ours.

At the end of the call, nothing was settled, and Fox continued using the name and advertising their FXTV channel, which was scheduled to launch in just three months.

Three months became two, and then it drained down to one short month … and something unexpected happened. Someone on their legal team must've woken up, realizing that they'd invested in a lot of marketing and promotion for their so-called FXTV, but they didn't own the name. And while that did spell FX, which was similar to Fox, minus the O, it also spelled potential trouble and headaches down the road.

In order to make it all right—and fast—they filed a lawsuit against us. Weeks away from launching a major national television channel, they couldn't leave anything to chance. Armed with a team of high-profile lawyers, they had their day in court, ready to claim what was rightfully ours.

Now, Alan and I didn't have an entire law firm on retainer. We did, however, have one lawyer, and it just so happened that he wasn't very expensive—or very good. We looked at him and said, "Listen, when you go in there, don't argue with them. Don't plead our case. Don't object or anything." Handing him a letter, we continued, "Just put this in your pocket. If the judge asks if you have anything to say, give him this letter. That's all you've got to do."

And that's exactly what he did. When the lawyers from Fox were done arguing their case, the judge asked our attorney if he had any evidence he wanted to present, and our responded by pulling out the letter and handing it to the judge.

After reading the letter, the judge actually laughed out loud.

The letter just so happened to be from the chairman of Fox. Like I said previously, it was friendly, but there was something even more significant about this particular letter for it was our entire case in defense of the accusations.

"Hey, Larry, it was great to see you … Good luck with FXTV."

With that, the judge turned to Fox's lawyers and pointed out that the chairman of their company didn't have any problem with us using the name FX; therefore, he suggested that the lawyers step out and try to negotiate a deal. In the end, Fox ended up paying us money to give up the FX name, which was pretty sweet, considering the fact that we were already convinced we weren't going to proceed with the channel.

Who knows? If they'd played nice and asked us kindly in the first place, we might've given them the name for free. But, hey, it put a few dollars in our pocket … and some much-needed confidence in our attorney. I'd say that was a win-win for everyone—well, except for Fox.

8 E!: A PLAN THAT SOMEHOW UNFOLDED

Naturally, the making of E! was complicated, so much that the process deserves a chapter of its own in this book. Alan and I came up with the idea for Entertainment Tonight 24 hours a day or MTV of the movies. We wrote a plan and were naïve enough to think that just because this all made sense to us, the money would follow. Unfortunately, it didn't work that way. Everyone told us it was a good idea, *but* they also pointed out that we weren't Time Inc. or a big studio, and regular people don't just start TV networks. That's for the big media companies. Lucky for us, I guess, we weren't smart enough to listen, so we didn't give up and just kept pushing along. It was a very interesting journey—one that entailed over 100 pitch sessions. And they were all pretty much the same. There were some who thought the idea wasn't very good and would say things like, "Do you really think people care about all this Hollywood stuff?" Then, there was the majority who said, "Nice idea but you aren't Rupert Murdock."

This is a good time to share some of the more interesting stories on our quest to get our first dollars.

Let me begin by saying that Alan had a few little quirks, and one was extreme anxiety attacks. When we were flying to NY from LA for a big meeting, we got on the plane and placed our bags in the overhead bins. The flight attendant came by, and we said hello and she moved on to the next row. Just a minute or two before the doors would close, Alan had an attack. He said, "I'm freaking out. I can't stay on the plane," and got up and ran off before they closed the doors.

We taxied out to the runway, and the same flight attendant came by and asked where my friend was. I explained he got off the plane abruptly, at which point, she went into a panic and ran to the cockpit. They turned the plane around and went back to the gate. I was immediately surrounded by the pilot, the flight attendant, and half a dozen security folks who ran onto the plane when we got to the gate. They grilled me as to who my friend was, how long I knew him, and asked if he left anything on the plane. I got a lot of very angry looks from the other passengers, who naturally assumed I was the cause of the flight delay. After satisfying the security folks that there was no danger and explaining that it was all due to Alan's panic attack, the plane departed. The dirty looks—well, they continued for the rest of the flight.

I later found out that Alan tried to catch the next flight out, only to be told the pilot notified the airline and Alan was banned for about a year from this airline. I, on the other hand, made it to NYC and conducted the meeting myself.

Alan was on another airline sometime after that, making small talk with a guy who sat next to him. Alan told him about our network idea, and the guy said that it was brilliant and asked when we were starting the network. Alan explained that we had no money, and the guy said that he was in charge of acquisitions and divestures for Warner Communication, and while this wasn't something for them, he knew some folks he thought would be interested. When Alan told me about this encounter, I met him in NYC, and we had a meeting with a bond house on Wall Street that had just started an investment banking division. They were looking for deals, and while this wasn't a thing they generally looked at, they agreed to meet with us. We met with Jeffrey Pollack, who was the newly made head of investment banking. After seeing a few posters on his wall, he explained that he was the entertainment reporter for his college newspaper and thought that the upside to what we were doing was huge. He agreed to invest 2.5 million dollars, and we took it. After all, we had been beating the bushes for three years. At this point, we'd take anything we could get.

The bond company was Mabon Nugent, and Jeffrey Pollack assigned one of his folks to be the lead on our project. They wanted to get a few small contributors who could provide not just money but strategic value to join in with them. Frank E Barnes, (known as Chip) was on the case, and he set up a bunch of meetings with funds who might be inclined to do a deal like ours.

One of the first meetings was with the family office of a famous American family. The office was in NYC, and for some reason, Alan was not able to make that meeting, so I took it with Chip. We sat in the conference room and waited 45 minutes for the managing director before he walked in, carrying a business plan. In those days, business plans were lengthy printed documents, and ours was about 200 pages with the financials. The first words out of his mouth were, "Who had the nerve to send me this piece of garbage?" and he just missed my head as he flung the plan across the room.

Being a street kid from Coney Island, I was not about to take that treatment, especially since I was sure he wasn't going to be an investor. So I went right back at him with a verbal attack and argument that lasted for about 15 minutes. When we were done, to my surprise, he got up from his chair, looked at Chip, and said, "I'm in, call me later to finalize this."

Then he walked out of the room without so much as a goodbye or a handshake. To this day, I'm not sure what happened to turn him around.

Eventually, Mabon got a group of investors to join them, and 2.5 million dollars was on its way. Among the group were the HC Crown Corp (the Hallmark Family), Hutton Small Cap Fund, Sidney Knafel and Michael Wilner, who ran some east coast cable system operations. This group eventually exited when we brought in several major cable companies in the next funding round.

CHAPTER 9

THE BLOODY BUTT THAT ALMOST DERAILED A NETWORK

The search for partners continued as Mabon was a little reluctant to go it alone. They had a few other small cap funds that expressed some interest and told us that one of them was serious but wanted to meet us at one of the national cable conventions in Texas. They said this was a very serious group, and we needed to be very buttoned up and professional—we being me, Alan, and Bruce, who was a partner at the time. Bruce was formerly with Showtime and was the person who connected me with Alan. Wanting everything to be perfect for the 9:00 a.m. meeting, we ordered just about everything on the menu from room service—bagels, toast, muffins, bacon, sausage, coffee, tea, and hot chocolate—and asked for everything to be brought to the room at 8:30 on the dot. Everything was perfect … except the fifth Beatle (as we called Bruce) had a white powder problem, and unknown to us, he had a rough night out with his cable buddies. Alan and I went into the bedroom to discuss how we were going to present our case and what we would say about our partner, who we thought was asleep. But when we came out, he was awake and had already hit the room service table and tasted everything. He literally took a bite out of everything on the table, and the crumbs were all over the place, including his face. To top it off, he spilled the coffee. Our plan was ruined. We moved the table into the hall and placed another order. The meeting time was drawing near, and we were scrambling when we noticed the fifth Beatle was planning on staying for the meeting.

Then, we noticed that we had yet another problem. The back of his pants were soaked with blood (from a hemorrhoid that had burst). Alan and I were in shock and were trying to push him into his bedroom when the doorbell rang. With no other choice, we made our partner sit on the couch and told him not to move or talk. We had just started the pitch when Bruce decided it was time for more coffee and got up. In an attempt to distract the potential investor, I danced over to the other side of the room, hoping his eyes would follow. Luckily, they did! But then Bruce started wandering around the room. For every move he made, I countered and went to another side of the room so the investor wouldn't see the blood-stained pants. Finally, Bruce sat down again, but when I looked over at the couch, it, too, was soaked with blood. Again, I danced around, hoping the investor's eyes would follow me. It was so crazy that he must have thought I was the one on drugs.

Somehow, we ended up managing to finish our pitch, and when the investor got up to leave, he said, "Okay, I get it. I'm in."

A little about Bruce: he was known as the fifth Beatle after he told us that our idea for a network was stupid and suggested we should take it down a notch and think about doing a TV show instead. He told us we could buy him out for 12k, and Alan did just that. After we launched, Bruce sued us, saying we should have convinced him this would be successful so he wouldn't sell. It was laughable. Even the judge laughed when he dismissed the case and placed a one-million-dollar bond requirement if he ever chose to pursue the lawsuit again.

Back to the convention. Our young assistant, Lisa, was also there. Lisa was a wild 19 year old, and Alan and I always marveled at her very open discussions about what she did the night before and who she slept with. Unfortunately, she partied a bit too hard and overdosed and died at the young age of 19.

It was a world that Alan and I were naïve to, but one which opened our eyes quickly. Sadly, we saw more than a few bright lives were impacted by drugs and the party atmosphere. Thankfully, we weren't sucked into that scene, although we lost an assistant and a partner, and there is a hotel out there that lost a couch.

CHAPTER 10 THE OJ STORIES

You probably recognize some of the names of the athletes who we partnered with when we were working on FXTV. There was Kareem, Bruce Jenner, and I think it's safe to say that just about everybody has heard of OJ Simpson. Well, here's the story about how we met … and my take on one of the biggest questions of the 90s: Did OJ get away with murder?

Hollywood is all about image and lifestyle, and while I lived and worked there, I was married and had two young kids and was more middle of the road, preferring a quieter out-of-the-public-eye lifestyle. Alan, on the other hand, was much more "Hollywood" than I was. And why not—he was a single guy living the life, going out on the town and frequenting all the local hot spots. At the time, he lived in LA in a great house in Coldwater Canyon and enjoyed dating young starlets, models, and Penthouse Pets.

Well, Alan called me one evening, and I could tell he was a bit frantic as he told me that he had to move out of his house, check into a hotel, and hire security. Apparently, he had made a very big guy very angry by going out with the big guy's girlfriend. For that, there would be a price to pay.

From what I could quickly gather—and later got all the details—Alan went out with a very hot young actress named Tawny Kitaen, who rose to fame as the female lead in the movie Bachelor Party and later married rockstar David Coverdale. Unknown to Alan at the time, Tawny was dating football legend OJ Simpson, who had a history of being pretty volatile.

Well, when the date was over, Alan was dropping Tawny off at her place, but when they were in front of her house, a car suddenly pulled up behind them. Seeing the car, Tawny knew who it was and told Alan not to stop his car and to drive around the block instead. As Alan drove around the block, they noticed that the car followed them. Once again, they didn't stop and went around the block one more time. The car stayed on their tail. Finally, Tawny said, "Stop the car. I'll get out and stand in front of his car. He won't run me over. You just drive away."

That's exactly what Alan did, but it didn't stop there. OJ had a score to settle, and it didn't have anything to do with football. A very angry OJ went to all the hotspots around town and let it be known that when he got his hands on Alan Mruvka, he was going to inflict pain—and lots of it.

Not one to let bygones be bygones, OJ wasn't going to give Alan an easy out. After several threatening phone exchanges, we thought of a way to hopefully calm him down and spare Alan's life (or at least keep him from beating him to a pulp). It seems Alan had a childhood friend named Blake Olson, whose father was Frank Olson, the Chairman of Hertz. Frank was the brainchild behind casting OJ in Hertz commercials, and in OJ's post-NFL days, his role as the Hertz spokesperson was very important to the running back. Along with his role as an NFL commentator, not only was it his most lucrative source of income, but the famous commercials featuring him running through airports were also what kept him in the center of the public eye. Alan either had to show his power or he was a dead man, so he let OJ know that if he didn't back off, all he had to do was call Blake and fill him in on what was going on—and he was certain that Blake would tell his dad. Because Frank Olsen was a deeply religious man, everyone knew that he wouldn't take too kindly to learning that his brand ambassador was going to beat up one of his son's friends—especially since OJ was married to Nicole Brown and cheating on her with Tawny, the woman OJ was willing to fight over.

When Frank Olson's name came into the picture, OJ quickly changed his tune and suggested that we all meet to clear this little matter up. After all, he said, there was no reason to let a gal cause any hard feelings or animosity between us. Understandably, Alan didn't want to go to this meeting alone, and he asked me to go with him to have lunch with OJ at La Scala Restaurant in Beverly Hills. We had a very nice, cordial lunch and, ironically, began a friendship and eventually a partnership in our potential network, FXTV.

Oh, I remember it well. I had the La Scala salad with salami.

Our friendship and partnership with OJ continued, and we got to know him well. OJ and Nicole would eventually divorce, and I also divorced my wife, the mother of my two children. A few days before Nicole Brown and Ron Goldman were murdered, I was with my then girlfriend, Nataly Sherbakova, at the Foundation Room of House of Blues. This was the private VIP room where all the Hollywood celebs hung out. By this time, I was a bit more "Hollywood," always loaded with young hot wannabe actresses, and, true to form, OJ was always working the room. But not on that night. Something was off, very off.

When I saw OJ, he was standing off to the side with his arms folded across his chest. He looked disturbed—almost ominous. Suffice it to say that there was no doubt that OJ was not happy. Concerned, I walked over to him and asked him if something was wrong. He clearly did not want to talk and shot back with, "Nothing, man," before returning to whatever it was that had disturbed him and was consuming his mind. Realizing that he was in no state of mind to make small talk, I left him alone for the rest of the night.

Even so, his mood stuck with me. It bothered me so much that I contacted Alan the next day for the sole purpose of seeing if he knew what was up.

"Hey, what's wrong with OJ?" I asked. "He was acting really weird last night."

Alan replied that he wasn't aware of anything, and we left it at that.

A few days later, I was in Moscow in my hotel room when a friend from LA called.

"Larry, do you get CNN?" he asked. "You need to turn it on."

Turning on the TV, I sat and watch the infamous "Bronco chase" from my hotel room in Russia.

It all came back to me—the way OJ had acted just a few nights before— the times Chris Jenner would ask me and Alan how we could possibly be friends with a guy who beats his wife. She even predicted it, saying that one day he could kill her. We dismissed her intuition, thinking she was an alarmist who was overprotective of Nicole, who was one of her very good friends.

That was the beginning of the downfall of OJ Simpson, as the murders took center stage over OJ's football career and accomplishments. Naturally, it was also the end of any potential partnership between me, Alan, and OJ.

And we all know how the saga ends as the life of one of football's greatest players took a downward spiral. But for a while, we got to know and work with The Juice—OJ Simpson—and actually became friends with the guy who threatened to tear Alan from limb to limb.

Ironically, Frank Olson and OJ Simpson both died on the very same day.

And to answer the question: yes, I believe OJ did it. In fact, I believe I interrupted him as he was creating his dark and sinister plan to do so when I asked if something was wrong.

While I knew that something wasn't right, little did I know that something was, indeed, wrong that night—something was very, very wrong.

11 THE WOMEN IN MY LIFE

As I mentioned in the previous chapter, at the time I met OJ, I was in a relationship with Nataly, but she was not the first serious relationship in my life. It would be impossible for me to write about the events and people in my life without introducing the women who were part of it. And it all started with Nancy.

Nancy was my high school sweetheart, and we literally were married right out of college. We were living in Brooklyn, and then together we moved to Manhattan. Our marriage unraveled about three years in, and the divorce was less than friendly. It's safe to say that it was bitter, and I admit that I was largely at fault. Time and hindsight have given me a new perspective, and I can see that I wasn't the best husband—actually, I was an idiot. Nancy was very hurt, and she became quite vindictive, and the divorce encompassed about four years in hearings and legal proceedings.

At the time of our divorce, I lived in California, while Nancy was in New York. And in my opinion, her lawyer was better than mine. Every time there was an issue, I'd have to go back to New York for a deposition. As you can imagine, after multiple depositions, flights, and time away from work, the fight wasn't worth the trouble and inconvenience. Finally, I just said, "You know what, we're fighting over money. You keep it all. I'm done."

Now, Nancy and I split before I came out to California, and I started seeing a woman who had worked at Manhattan Cable. Our relationship started right before I moved to California, and Carolyn joined me after I started working for Valley. Carolyn and I had two children, Nicole and Jonathan. And when that relationship ended, I met Nataly, who was the niece of the former Russian ruler, Leonid Brezhnev.

At the time, Nataly was living here, but she grew up in Russia and was kind of like a little princess. After all, she had a powerful uncle—the kind of uncle who could send people to Siberia, never to be seen again.

Nataly is the mother of my youngest son, Alexander.

As most people know, the entertainment industry isn't always conducive to lasting relationships, and I can (partly) contribute the demise of these relationships to the environment. But I do not regret those relationships. They were important parts of my life—and I've learned a great deal from them. Even more, though, through these relationships, I became a father, and I love and am proud of all my children and the grandchild they have given me who has enriched my life and brought me joy.

Most of all, my relationships taught me that the most important thing in life is to be happy. I'm not quite sure where I got that insight, but I used to argue it with my mom. She would say, "Are Nicole and her boyfriend serious and planning to get married?" My response was always the same: "I don't care if she gets married, just that she is happy."

The object is not to be married but to be happy, and if marriage helps you reach that state, so be it. If not, and that is what makes you happy, be content with being single.

CHAPTER 12 TO RUSSIA, WITH LOVE

While E! was a challenge to fund and launch, it became a huge success and was the birthplace for some long-time shows, like Talk Soup, Howard Stern, E! Hollywood True Stories, Wild on E!, and Fashion Police with Joan Rivers. People loved having a window into the world of the stars, and our platform gave them access to their idols and allowed them to see the lives of celebrities from the outside in. We enjoyed our success, which sparked interested buyers. Eventually, Alan and I sold our stake in E!, though I remained on the board of directors.

I was contemplating my next move when a lawyer friend called and said he had some clients involved in merchant banking. It seemed that he had a connection in the Soviet Union who proposed an entertainment deal to them. He asked if I would go to Russia with them and see if this deal had any validity. Totally intrigued with the thought of going to the Soviet Union, I quickly agreed.

Now, at the time, I didn't know a lot about Russia, but I remember back in public school PS 188 in Brooklyn, that we frequently had air raid drills and had to get under our desks in the event that the Soviets bombed us.

It started with Khruschev pounding his shoe on the podium of the UN and then was taken on by his successor, Leonid Brezhnev.

I went to Moscow and then on to St. Petersburg with them, where I met a Russian general who was seeing the future and had dreams of starting a film company. He and Tom Wheelock, one of the merchant banking folks, met in the Sinai Desert when Russia and the US both supplied UN peace-keeping forces. As I remember their stories, they patrolled the borders during the day and drank vodka at night. I went with them, and the idea they were presented with was not very good. It was about creating a company that would build living room facilities around the country that people could rent to show VHS movies on a big screen via a projector. We passed on that deal, but I met Anatoly Sobchak, the mayor of St. Petersburg, who convinced me that the move to rid the country of Communists was inevitable and Russia would join the world as a democracy.

I have to say that the whole thing was surreal, much like I was living within a piece of history. It was exciting to meet the folks we had considered our enemy for so many decades, only to find out we had so much in common. We all had dreams for our lives, our children, and our freedom. As a matter of fact, there is one saying that I heard over and over that stuck with me. "America is what we would have been if it wasn't for the f'n communists."

Now, when I went to Russia, it was still the Soviet Union, and the state-run machines were l in full force, although you could sense that their time was soon to expire. The people were wonderful, and even with food shortages and other hardships, they would invite people into their home and make them tea. If they had to, they would empty the refrigerator in order to be a good host.

I ultimately decided to partner with the merchant bankers, and we started a new company called Comspan Communications, whose sole mission was to build business in Russia. Tom and his partner, Lou, mainly handled the merchant banking stuff, while I handled my areas of expertise: media and entertainment. After Lou left the company, Tom and I shared all the responsibilities, along with David Lafaille, the lawyer who approached me about going there who came in as counsel to the new company.

We worked very closely with a St. Petersburg company called Russian Video, which was headed by a very philosophical Russian named Dimitri Rozhdeshevsky, who was a wonderful, brilliant guy but a dreamer on steroids. On top of that, he talked in long metaphors—saying hello to him often turned into an hour-long conversation. He was full of grandiose ideas on building a media empire, but sometimes he forgot this was still the Soviet Union and the chances of that happening were slim, very slim. But I have to admit that it was fun to dream with him, and we did some very fun stuff together, like making a movie called Russian Holiday, which was essentially the classic Roman Holiday but set in St. Petersburg. Actually, it was a terrible movie, but we managed to sell it to CBS at a profit. For me, that was a humbling lesson—one where I learned what I'm not good at. It turns out that I am not good at making movies.

The best thing to come out of the Russian video experience was making a lifelong friendship with Oganes Sobolev, the head of business development. Oganes and I became fast friends, and I met his family—his wife, Karen, and their son, Sasha. They lived in a tiny two-room apartment in Moscow. Not only was money a problem in Russia then, but even if you had it, it didn't mean you could find things to buy. For instance, finding winter garb for young Sasha was very challenging, and I would often load my suitcase with clothes for him and bring them to Moscow.

They were undoubtedly tough times, but Oganes and his friends started a company called Video International, which became the largest seller of ad time on Russian national channels. They eventually sold out to a Kremlin insider for several billion dollars. Recently, Oganes and his family moved out of Russia due to the chaos of the Ukraine situation.

When I decided to put a lot of time and effort into what was then the Soviet Union, we formed a close alliance with Russian Video, and one of the benefits was that it was based out of the complex they had on a private island in St. Petersburg. An amazing place, it was the former summer house of many of the elites within the Communist party. To give you a picture, it was about 10,000 square feet on a river (with a boat dock) and came with 5 household workers, including a full-time cook. There was a downside, though—one of the former horse stables was the monitoring station for the KGB, and every room had listening devices. I admit that was scary at first, but I soon got used to it. I'd even sneak down to the stables and surprise the listeners and offer them cigarettes. It seemed that the most important currency you could have there were Marlboro Reds and women's panty hose.

While it was still the Soviet Union, there was a crazy thing they called the five-year plan. This would mandate what farmers could plant and harvest and when. Whenever I would ask for something specific, the response would always be, "That's in deficit." On the other hand, when it was chicken month, chicken was in abundance … but nothing else was available. Now, I'll admit that I had a huge problem with tongue month. My lips don't touch tongue … unless it's attached to a woman.

Frankfurter month was also a nightmare, and I quickly learned that I had a big problem with the house workers, who saw me as an ungrateful capitalist pig. One day, I got a frankfurter and roast potatoes for breakfast, and I admit that I was very suspicious of what goes into a Soviet frankfurter. (I'm a Nathan's all-beef guy to this day.) So I was leery about eating it and chose to eat only the potato and leave the frank untouched. Lo and behold, that same frankfurter appeared on my lunch plate, but this time, it was hidden in a slice of bread (Soviet's version of a hot dog bun). I ate the cucumber that came on the side and the bread … but not the frank. Guess what? The frank came back on my dinner plate, this time chopped into little pieces and mixed into mashed potato so I couldn't pick it out. Lesson learned. That's how they teach a lesson to an ungrateful capitalist pig, I guess. From then on, I would bring an extra suitcase filled with things like instant oatmeal or other "just add water" foods so I wouldn't go hungry or have to relegate my health to whatever unknown food they put on my plate.

13 THE SOVIET UNION, ST. PETE, AND SANTA BARBARA

The dissolution of the Soviet Union brought with it many problems. Without central authority to at least demand farmers grow or raise certain foods, it was pure chaos. Food shortages wracked the country, and it was quite common to see people standing in lines for hours to get anything that was available. At the dacha (the house we lived in), things were a little better. We didn't get a wide variety of food, but they made sure we did get something to eat three times a day.

Things changed when I brought a hit TV show to China and made friends with all the politicians, as well as the big mafia guys, who seemed to have access to lots of the stuff that was supposedly in deficit.

The woman who ran the house was a holdover from the glory days of the Communist party rule. She was used to the top of the party elite staying there and was clearly not very happy about having to host this capitalist pig. There were times when we'd throw parties there, and, believe me, she would go nuts. At one party, we brought back a bunch of the local girls for some drinking and dancing. There was one room that had a billiard table, and one of the girls thought it would be funny to dance on Brezhnev's billiard table. We got reported to the local party officials, who asked Rozdeshvensky to PLEASE (with a great deal of emphasis) ask us to behave. That's when we realized that this was going to become one of the greatest party cities on the planet, joining Prague and Budapest—eventually, though, Moscow eclipsed St. Petersburg as the best party city.

It wasn't all parties, though. We lived through tumultuous times there, when Gorbachev was in charge and then got run off and replaced by Yeltsin. Tom was there when the shit the fan, and there was a coup. At the time, he was in the Ukraine hotel in Moscow, where he had a great view as everything unfolded. The tanks rolled through the streets of Moscow, and it was then that the famous photo of Yeltsin standing in front of the military tanks was taken. The genie was out of the bottle, and the Communist party rule was dismantled. Following very closely on its heels was the fall of the entire Soviet Empire as each part of the Soviet Union declared their independence from Moscow rule.

The biggest issue was that with the fall of the central government, it was the folks with the smallest voices who got screwed the most, particularly the children and the elderly.

But in the case of me and Tom, the business opportunities were never more apparent.

The Mayor of St. Petersburg, Mr. Sobchak was a reformer, and he not only wanted to improve the lives of the folks in his city, but he also believed in democratic ideals. In addition, he made it clear that he wanted to maintain St. Petersburg's history as a cultural center of the eastern bloc. That's when we saw our window of opportunity and started to really delve into bringing western culture to the country. It started with some small film festivals featuring films from around the world, and it eventually grew to be a full-fledged effort on our side. The biggest thing we did, around the year 1991, was to bring the American soap opera to Russia and the republics (via the national TV network that was still operating throughout). Because we were boots on the ground, we were very in touch with Russian people and not just politicians. As a result, we had a better feel for what could be popular. For example, while most American companies thought that high profile shows like Dallas would be big hits, we had a different take. By talking to everyday people, we became aware of an odd (for us) take on the Dallas story line: "Why would two brothers fight over money?" was what we were hearing. Coming out of 72 years of Communism, the Russians couldn't understand family feuds over things like money. On the other hand, the place was falling apart, and life was very hard. People wanted to go home after a hard day and forget their problems. Vodka was one way, but soap operas were another. Knowing that, we made a deal to bring the show Santa Barbara to Russia. The owners of the show had zero revenue from the territory, and the head of New World, Jim McNamara, was very keen on getting the show to start generating revenue there. Working with the newly formed Video International agency, we got it on the number one TV station. At first. the dubbing was done by just one person narrating the story. Instead of dubbing in Russian, though, he would say, "He said or she said." In Soviet times, no Soviet films shown in the theaters would have a narrator behind the screen explaining the story in real time. We realized that getting advertisers involved in supporting this low-level attempt at content creation would be difficult, so we insisted on actually dubbing the voices and using the original dialogue. Their answer was to have one man and one woman do all the voices. While I have rarely been accused of having too much artistic integrity, this was too much for me. We finally got our way, and different voice actors played the different characters.

The show was a huge hit, and just as we suspected, people saw it as a great way to escape the problems of life in those hard times. It was watched every night by families joined together in front of a TV set wherever they can find one—the only competition the show ever had was a Mexican soap opera called The Rich also Cry. The sheer power of the show was unimaginable—actually, I'd never seen anything like it.

When Yeltsin wanted to preempt the show one night so he could give a political address, the people literally threatened to burn down the White House. If you went to a store to shop in the evening, it wasn't unusual to find that the folks who worked in the store had locked the doors so they could watch the show. People lined up outside the shops, waiting for the show to be over. It was a massive hit that aired five days a week for ten years. In the early years, it would garner 80 percent of all the homes watching television. Even to this day, when I meet Russians anywhere in the world, they remember watching the show with their families.

There is even a famous joke about it. "So Vladamir, I hear you are going on a trip to the US. Where will you visit?"

And Vladimir replies, "I'm going to New York, Las Vegas, and Santa Barbara."

"Santa Barbara, why?"

Vladamir replies, "Well, I already know everybody there!!!"

Television sets in the Soviet era were dangerous, not just because of the party propaganda but also because they had a tendency to explode. In the 90s, Russia would experience 50 or so deaths by television each year.

The power of the show went well beyond that. With the fall of central government and police governance came the rise of what was known as Sportmeni, which was the early version of the organized crime families that came to being. They were strong and tough, and they could fight. Since guns were not yet a regular thing in the market, hand-to-hand fighting was the main force of power. The entrance of guns that were strictly forbidden before changed things for the worse. Instead of just getting beat up, people were getting shot to death.

While Russia was undergoing so many changes, Santa Barbara changed my life in Russia. For one thing, all of the mob guys had girlfriends who were avid fans of the show. Of course, they knew who I was; it was pretty obvious I was the Hollywood guy who lived at the dacha. I could be sitting in a restaurant when one would walk up to me and ask me to "tell me what happens to Mason in next week's episodes so I can impress my girlfriend (or wife)." When I would first say I can't divulge that kind of information, they would make me an offer I couldn't refuse (not in godfather terms), like "If you tell me, we know where to get fresh tomatoes and we will bring them to you." I told, and every week a delivery of fresh produce would miraculously show up at the dacha.

Then there was the time that I thought I would have a heart attack. The main guys who ran St. Petersburg and beyond knew me, and I knew them. You could say that we had a friendly relationship of sorts. I was not seen as the American carpetbagger who came to Russia to make a quick buck. Rather, I was seen as someone who had an interest in helping the people of the city I came to love, and they didn't believe that profit was my only motive. At the time, the city bosses had enormous power and were known to be very brutal to defend their turf. One time when I flew into St. Pete, cars drove up to the plane, which I found odd. Generally, back then, planes parked on the runway, and buses would take the passengers to the terminals. But this was different. I came down the stairway to a half a dozen guys, who were looking at something and talking to each other. To my surprise, the thing they were looking at was my picture. "Are you Larry Namer?" they asked. I said yes … but in a very nervous way. In response, they told me to get in the car. They drove me back to the terminal building and walked me to customs. The line was probably an hour long, but they went right to the front and told the customs officer, "He is with us," and we walked right through.

Then they told me that their boss needed to see me at 8 p.m. that night at the Astoria Hotel. To say I was nervous would be an understatement—and for good reason: the boss was known to be a very dangerous guy. I couldn't imagine what he wanted from me, but my imagination came up with some pretty terrifying possibilities. Someone who worked for me insulted him, and they want me to kill that person? They had a spat with the mayor and know I'm having dinner with him and they are going to plant a gun for me to find and shoot him? (This came from the scene in The Godfather where Michael shoots the enemy of his father and the crooked cop.) I was beyond nervous the more I thought about why he could possibly want to see me. I was waiting outside the hotel when a parade of cars drew up. First came the big guys in Armani suits with pistols clearly bulging, then the boss followed. He spoke a little English, and I spoke a little Russian, but one of his folks spoke both fairly well and facilitated the exchange. The boss put his arm around my shoulders and started walking into the hotel with me in tow (he was very strong). "We need to talk," he said. I wasn't about to argue, but I thought my legs would give out. Then he said, "I'm embarrassed to ask this, but I need a favor."

"You name it, you got it," I somehow managed to reply, thinking this might be what I needed to say to spare my life. He repeated that he was embarrassed to ask for this favor, but he must. Then he continued. "I heard that at your concert tomorrow night you have the actor who plays Mason in Santa Barbara coming as a special guest. My mother is the show's biggest fan, and I would be very grateful if there was some way you could introduce her to Mason" (played by actor Lane Davies). I almost collapsed in relief, but somehow found my bearings and said, "Sure, bring mom to the back door of the concert hall at 8 p.m., and I'll take her to the VIP room and introduce her to Lane."

When I saw Lane, I told him that I was going to introduce him to the prettiest woman he'd ever met and he needed to be especially nice and gracious. He thought I was nuts, and I don't blame him, but I told him that he didn't want to know the story. "Just do as I say."

The next night, they showed up as scheduled, and I walked them both up to the VIP room. She was a very nice little Russian lady, who was also a school official. Now, I should mention that my security at the concert and in the VIP room were all well-trained Russian security forces and police. When they saw who came into the room with me, they immediately left. I brought his mom over to Lane, and he hugged her as the photographers took pictures. The boss stood against the back wall with arms folded and a blank look on his face, so I couldn't tell what he was thinking. Then the mom presented Lane with a special proclamation that was created by some students and told him that he had brought such joy into so many lives. When it was all over, I walked her back to her son, who just looked at me and said, "You made my mother very happy, I never forget." From that day forward, my life in St. Peterburg changed dramatically. It seems he sent my picture with his folks to every restaurant and night club in town and instructed the folks who ran those places that it didn't matter if I was drunk at 3 a.m. and walking alone with a $100 bill taped to my forehead, they were responsible for getting me home safely. If I as much as hit a bump in a taxi, they would have to answer to the boss. No matter where I went, people would come up and ask me if everything was okay and if there was anything they could do for me.

I was at a restaurant with my friend, Michael, from the US, and some of the boys came up and asked if everything was okay. They even told us not to worry about paying for the meal—everything was taken care of. Michael asked where we could go to find girls, as he pointed to a few sitting at a table with their boyfriends (or husbands), saying we wanted to go somewhere to find girls like that. They went to the table and had a discussion with the people, and it was clearly obvious that the guys with the girls were not happy. And who could blame them? It seems they told the girls that they needed to leave these guys and come to our table. The girls were locals and understood this was not a simple ask, but rather an order. On the contrary, the guys were not locals, and they kept arguing and objecting. When we were leaving the place to go to a nightclub with the girls, the guys followed … but so did the St. Pete boys. A fight broke out—the bloodiest beating I ever witnessed. I could literally hear bones cracking. Those poor guys were on the receiving end of what I had feared was going to happen to me when I was approached by the St. Pete boys.

But somehow in a strange twist of fate, they were beating the pulp out of other people in order to take care of me. And I have to tell you that the boss kept his promise—it was like that everywhere I went. I had my own personal security guards, and the St. Pete boys made sure I got whatever I wanted, no matter what.

CHAPTER 14 — THE BEAUTY OF IT ALL

St. Petersburg was still Leningrad when I first started going there during the Soviet days. When it changed its name back to St. Petersburg, someone thought it would be a good idea to have a beauty contest — Miss St. Petersburg. To me, this was comical. After all, I grew up during the cold war, and all I knew about Russia was our own propaganda. The commercials on TV depicted Russian women in a different light, as BIG women in bathing suits pulling plows. So, that's what I envisioned Russian women to be. "Strong, like ox." Boy, was I wrong. What I saw in real life were some of the most beautiful women I've ever seen. That was true for more than Russia — you couldn't walk down the street in the former Soviet republics or Eastern Europe without falling in love.

I was asked to be a judge in that first beauty contest, and, of course, I agreed. It was interesting. For one thing, the host was dressed as Peter the Great, and the "entertainment" was a dancing bear. Okay, they hadn't done this sort of thing in a while, so I guess this was a good first attempt. Now when we got to the judging, that was a whole new experience for me. As Dorothy said in The Wizard of Oz, "We are not in Kansas anymore."

I was diligently reviewing the pictures and information about all the contestants when a few guys with twisted noses walked over to me and showed me a picture of one contestant. "This is the winner," they said. And who was I to argue?

The next year, the organizers wanted to raise the bar and asked me to bring supermodel Claudia Shiffer to be a judge. We did as asked, and she was a judge. The following year, it was Linda Evangelista, and the next year it was Wonder Bra girl, Eva Herzigova. Through it all, I was liking Russia more and more.

After my breakup with Nataly, a friend in LA introduced me to a model from the Ukraine who was one of the faces of Loreal for Eastern Europe. She was by far the most beautiful person inside and out I have ever met. We lived together for a year, and she was amazing in so many ways. She couldn't understand why I had a maid come in to clean the house when she could do it herself. She didn't do drugs, and as beautiful as she was, she had no ego. She was just a sweet, warm, wonderful person who was so happy to be out of the Ukraine and living in LA. Even my mother liked her, saying she was the first woman I was with who called her "mom." Unfortunately, she needed to get married in order to stay here, and I was not ready to get remarried. So we parted and a matchmaker connected her to a tech millionaire who was thrilled to have a bride like her. He moved her out of LA for fear she would reconnect with me or someone else and would be influenced by her friends (most from Russia or eastern Europe). Living in isolation in Northern California, she became depressed and was prescribed anti-depressants. She had a daughter and seemed to be suffering from post-partum depression on top of it. The daughter was three when I got a call from Dianne, the matchmaker who connected her to her husband who informed me Tetyana had died in her sleep. She said it was a reaction to the pills and wine, but I never found out more.

To this day, I want to kick myself in the butt for not marrying her. I've never met anyone like her and doubt I ever will … you could say she is the one who got away. And I'm the one who let her go.

15 THE CHINA YEARS

It's unbelievable, but this college graduate who wanted to be a teacher went from Coney Island to Los Angeles. Yes, it was a bit of a culture shock. Naturally, that shock intensified when I went to the Soviet Union, and to my surprise, later to China. One thing I did in Russia was help the Minister of Communications write the new policies for governing television and media in general. Michael Lessin was the minister but before that, he was the head of Video International, the company we worked with to bring Santa Barbara to Russia. The Russians realized that to build a consumer economy, they would have to make advertising media somewhat familiar to western marketers. I helped with that, and when the Chinese came to that same conclusion, they went to the Russians, who sent them to me.

We started in China with the low-hanging fruit. Our first show was called Hello Hollywood, and because we didn't speak the language, we had a Mandarin-speaking person in LA go to all the parties and premiers and interview the stars.

At the time, the landscape in China's TV scene was beginning to change dramatically as they moved toward building a consumer economy. Each of the major regions in China had their own media group which ran multiple channels. For example, Beijing had BTV *Beijing TV," and Shanghai had SMG (Shanghai Media Group). For me, this started to feel very familiar, much like the early days of US cable where certain media companies became the developers of multiple thematic channels.

It stayed that way in China until the government passed new rules that allowed each regional media company to put one of their channels up on satellite and distribute it all over the country. While satellite technology allowed the new signal to have a country-wide footprint, it still required each satellite channel to make a deal with another regional media company to carry that channel. This resembled how the channel business in the US rolled out, only it was a bit more orderly. When we started Movietime (E!), we put the signal on satellite but then had to go from city to city to convince the local cable company to add us to their line-up. There were hundreds of important, big companies and thousands of smaller rural companies, so I spent a great deal of my time on the road pitching cable operators. They were all different, but as you can imagine, they all seemed like Déjà vu to me.

Even with the growth of satellite TV, it was quite a challenge to get on a national feed. This was all new to them, and there weren't a lot of sources where they could turn for data to support our pitches for getting programs on. BUT, once again drawing on my past life, we found an opportunity in the marketplace with something that was very common in the US but not yet explored in China—Syndicated Television. The local stations were now having to supplement the government-provided funding by actually getting an audience that could be defined and measured, and then they had to sell advertising to brands looking to reach that audience. For the local stations, it was especially difficult because they had to compete with the bigger national channels to get the best program, as well as the advertisers that wanted those audiences. So we decided to bring the concept of syndication to the market.

We created the Hello Hollywood show at a production level worthy of national distribution, but we went to each of the local TV stations and got them to agree to carry the show in exchange for allowing us to sell national advertising. We ended up with over 40 stations signing on and had a reach of a few hundred million homes. Not too shabby.

The next challenge was piracy, which at the time was rampant in the market. This media for profit world was all new, and there was not a body of law that effectively protected ownership like that which exists in most of the world. The government was actually actively enacting laws in an attempt to stop piracy, but, because they were new, the enforcement was yet to catch up. With Hello Hollywood, we soon found out that for as many stations that had signed a real license with us, there were pirate operations that were showing our show without any license at all.

Rather than beat our heads against the wall trying to stop the piracy, we took a lesson from Abbie Hoffman, who wrote *Steal This Book*, and we called the pirates (who were easy to find) and said that we would not report them to the government on one condition: They had to wait two days from when we first broadcast the episode before they offered it up, and they had to report to us the viewership numbers in a format we specified. This increased our viewership, which in turn we sold to advertisers and made money from the audience the pirates delivered. The pirates were happy to get a high-quality show for free with just the simple task of staying out of legal trouble. For all of us, it was a win-win.

When we started Metan Global Entertainment, we built a strong team in a very deliberate way. In Los Angeles, we opened an office and took in interns from the local universities, including USC, UCLA, Pepperdine, and Loyola. We only took folks who were born and raised in Mainland China and wanted to return there after graduation. From that select group, we took the best and brightest and gave them entry-level jobs. From there, they returned to China and the best went to work in our

Beijing office. So we had a team of not only bilingual but, more important, bicultural folks. This was invaluable in helping me learn how to create for a country and culture I didn't grow up in.

That really came in to play when we created several original shows for China. The first was Modern Life, which I would describe as Friends Meets Big Bang Theory. Take the Friends concept and modernize it so there are cell phones and the Internet, and then put it into a new show where being a nerd was cool. (Okay, so Ross was kind of nerdy on Friends, but I'm talking about the whole cast of characters.) The business goal was to help Bacardi (the liquor company) expand their brand messaging by integrating them into the story.

Unfortunately, their message was too complex to get across in a regular television ad slot. For one thing, China didn't have much history insofar as mixed drinks. You went to a restaurant and the waiter would bring you a beer or rice wine. That was usually it. But Bacardi smartly realized that the Chinese in general liked to drink, and they figured if they could expose them to mixed drinks, the opportunity in the market was huge. To do this, they would build bartending schools and train a new generation of bartenders in making mixed drinks. It was a good idea, but they faced yet another problem. Apparently, being a bartender was not a profession that Chinese folks aspired to, so we had to get that point across when creating the story. In our show, one of the "friends" discovered bartender school and decided to go. In each episode, he returned home from classes and told the others about everything he learned. Now, he never made a drink in the show. We just built him up to be an expert in western cocktails and then had him show "the how" part either on the website or at restaurant or club openings where Bacardi would be the liquor provider.

I have to admit that getting the China brand team to understand subtlety was a challenge for our team. They thought that a Bacardi bottle should be visible in every scene, and they went so far to think it should have been sitting on the nightstand when we showed one of the characters who was just waking up. Thank goodness, we prevailed, and product placement was kept to a bare minimum.

We ran the ten episodes on some of the biggest digital platforms where we would reach the most affluent, educated, urban audiences. The series drew over 50 million viewers, and while we can't take total credit for making mixed drinks a regular part of Chinese life, we certainly can claim some of the credit.

It became clear early on that not all of our non-Chinese executives were suited for very unstructured environments, like the China media scene was in the early years of the transition. While we hired seasoned folks who had good backgrounds that came out of big agencies, most were not able to adapt to the environment. Frankly, the people, money and other resources were nowhere near the levels they were used to. It takes an entrepreneurial spirit to survive a start-up and even more than that to survive a start-up in another culture and country.

Thus far, I'd say that the biggest hit we have had in China has been Return to the Village of Good Fortune. One of the most interesting things we did within that series was take a position against shark finning. Generally, we stay away from political statements, but some things are too big to simply ignore. For a little background, the Chinese are known for eating just about every kind of animal and every part of it, but when it comes to shark fin, they do something astounding. Serving shark fin soup at a family affair such as a wedding is a status symbol and an expression of wealth and well-being reserved for very few. Only an elite group could afford it. However, in the past 30 years as China prospered and more people joined the middle and upper class, the serving of shark fin soup remained a demonstration of newfound prosperity. The only difference was that now there were hundreds of millions of people who could afford it. This caused a problem—before long, the number of sharks killed for their fins exceeded 80 million in a year. The whole thing was puzzling to me. For one thing, I didn't think shark fin had any real flavor whatsoever, and second, I discovered that they'd catch the sharks, cut off and keep the fin, then they would toss the disabled shark back in the water. Why they didn't keep it and eat it made no sense at all.

In an attempt to tiptoe around the issue, the young kids in our series were purposely very environmentally conscious (as I found most young people in China to be), so they were appalled when Grandma wanted to serve shark fin soup at her birthday celebration. As a solution, they found a chef in Beijing who created faux sharks fin soup out of chicken bones, and they had him make the soup, which actually fooled their grandma and all of her guests. I guess the show had an impact, because not long after that, hotels in some of the big cities decided to stop serving sharks fin soup.

On one trip out of Beijing to a city in western China, I was served what I thought looked like popcorn shrimp. It had a sweet and sour sauce and tasted quite good, except the texture was very gelatinous. When I inquired as to what it was. I was surprised to learn that I had a plate of battered and fried chicken knees in front of me. I didn't even know chickens had knees, but, more important, I wanted to figure out how to get the good parts of the chicken.

Another of my least favorite things to eat in China was pig's ear salad. Yeeech. I don't think I need to say more.

While I never grew accustomed to pig's ear salad, one custom I caught on to rather quickly was their way of conducting business. Whenever I went to a meeting with a TV station or media group, it inevitably started out well and was productive. Then when we reached the point of agreeing to do business together, another "executive" would enter the meeting (always wearing a bad gray suit), and he would listen to what we were agreeing to and then give it his blessing. The meeting would always end with him inviting me out to dinner and drinks. Since respect and tradition are so important in China, I could never refuse. So, we would go out (usually me and Jean, our business partner) and then get invited to a drinking dinner. On their side, there would be four or five people who would toast "the honored guest." Here's how it went down. When we made a toast, they would have one drink, but individually they would toast us, and we found ourselves having five for their one.

I think the funniest time was when my Russian friend and Metan Global Entertainment investor, Oganes, was at the meeting with me and, of course, joined us for dinner. Before we headed down to the restaurant, I explained that I had a very bad allergy to alcohol and the doctor said if my lips even touch liquor, I could die. But I went on to tell them that my friend, Oganes, "is from Russia, and he has been drinking since birth. He would be happy to drink all night with you." What I found amazing was that even at five to one, Oganes outdrank them. I guess there is a lot to be said for starting young.

We had a lot of successes in China, and through our connections, we were able to bring them more than television shows. For one thing, we brought the Harlem Globetrotters to China for several exhibitions in Macau. One of the most successful things we did, though, was bring the Leonardo Da Vinci exhibition to China. This was an exhibition created in Milan, and it did very well in China. That led us to believe that immersive exhibitions like Van Gogh or 100 Years of Disney Animation would do very well, so we refocused our efforts a bit to negotiate territory licenses for those and cut back on producing original content (but still do that).

While Covid but a crimp on our China activities, we managed to survive by shifting our focus from production (which is impossible to do during lockdowns and quarantines) to other things, like creating a company that would source goods from Chinese factories on behalf of western companies, who typically had to go through brokers and pay huge markups. Since we had good people who spoke English, a Beijing office, and strong knowledge of the Chinese manufacturing scene, we used this detour to generate enough revenue to keep us alive during the very difficult time.

The pandemic was challenging for everyone, and I wasn't an exemption. In 2020, when Covid was making its appearance, I started developing again in the States—this time, under the banner of LJN Media Group.

CHAPTER 16 — MY MICROSOFT DAYS

One day, we got a call from someone at Microsoft who said they wanted to meet with me to discuss a new technology related to media and entertainment that Bill Gates was solidly behind. He explained that he got our information from Rick Portin, who was the head of production at E! but was now back living in the Seattle area and working as a consultant to Microsoft on production issues. They needed someone who understood the media world at a high level, someone they could trust to tell them what was best for Microsoft, someone who didn't have any other agenda. Rupert Murdoch was telling them to follow him into the future, John Malone from TCI was doing the same, and then, of course, so was Time Warner. Hearing what they had to say, we signed on at first to provide advice and guidance on navigating the media world, as well as working with a part of the Windows team who needed to understand how TV people might use interactivity.

This all fell under a group called MiTV, which reported to a long-time Microsoft person named Paul Mitchell. While people were quick to criticize Microsoft for all sorts of things, we had nothing but good experiences (well, almost nothing, but we will get to that later). For me, this was a really great opportunity. I consider myself a creative, but my college degree was economics. For that reason alone, I was an oddity in Hollywood. Being a creative who understood a balance sheet was not common back then. Now, I was expanding my knowledge, getting lessons in technology and the development of the things that drive the future of all industries. So, I guess you could say I was becoming a triple threat.

I found that Microsoft had an amazing way of identifying and recruiting the smartest kids on the planet. They lived and breathed their jobs, and it was common to find some of them sleeping on the floor in the morning after spending the previous night problem solving. We played with the idea of what was called enhanced TV. Now, keep in mind that this was in the days before digital TV and when dial-up Internet was the primary way to get online. The premise was fairly simple: What if you could overlay a web browser on top of a TV picture and use that as a way of adding more information? As we went deeper into the creative uses of this concept, it became clear that we could do quite a lot. What if you could overlay several browsers with the number increasing every time someone watched the same TV show? You could change the overall experience and give people new reasons to come back.

For example, I'm a Seinfeld fan and have seen every episode several times, so I don't have a lot of reasons to watch anything but my favorite episodes. But what if the system knew I was watching again, and the browser contained anecdotes from Jerry himself about what went on the day they filmed that episode, or it contained jokes that didn't make it into the final edit? As a fan of the show, I would watch every episode again. Then maybe the next time I would get anecdotes from Elaine, then George, and then Kramer. I would watch it over and over because the experience would be different. It would be new. Since TV reruns are the big profit centers for the show creators, networks, etc., this not only enhanced the fan experience but also enhanced the monetary value of the show itself.

As we contemplated the possibilities, we got to really stretch our minds as to what could be done. It went beyond entertainment. There were implications for education, health and wellness, and many other things. For example, as a writer, I might write something targeted for adults, but what if the show was watched by a teen who didn't know the vocabulary I was using or the references I was making? Someone who fit the profile I created this for didn't need anything more from me, but what if there was a small button on the side of the screen that let the viewer know there was more to be had if they clicked it? It could be an explanation of a reference or just a definition of a term. Whatever it was, this technology could broaden the accessibility and enjoyability of the show. Knowing that, a team was assigned to build TV functionality into the operating system. Most people would never know it was there, but we could get a base of users to start interacting with the enhancements we would provide. To broaden the test audience, Microsoft looked into buying a company called WEBTV, which built stand-alone boxes that attached to your cable and a telephone line and enabled the same content enhancements. We wanted to work with the creators and writers of the series, so the idea of the enhancements would be baked into the show itself. However, convincing TV networks was not an easy thing, as they were all fearful of Microsoft. Even so, we did find some brave souls and did some very interesting stuff.

First up was enhancing Baywatch (no pun intended), which was geared to a relatively younger audience. But I thought it wasn't going to be difficult to know what can be done for the younger folks, so I wondered what we could do to attract an older and less tech-savvy user. After trying to convince many show owners and talents, we hit upon a very unlikely show, Judge Judy. Judy was very frank and said that while she didn't necessarily understand everything we were talking about, she knew the future of TV was changing and she wanted to stay on top of everything new. In the end, we worked closely with a guy named David Feinlieb, who was amazing and turned our creative ideas into functional features, and we did over 200 enhanced episodes of the show, using it as a way for viewers to purchase her new book just by clicking a link. The biggest surprise was how older folks were using the chat function more than anything else. This was a way to provide shared experiences with their friends and relatives and a way to combat loneliness. I used my mom as a guinea pig, so I could get constant feedback. She loved the chat and would use it to connect to her friends all over the country as they watched the show together. I realized that this was no different than me watching a New York Giants football game and calling my friends to discuss how bad the coaching or players were—with one difference: this was easier.

The next big thing we tried to do was called Simulchat, where we created an in studio that would watch certain shows at certain times and comment about the show. There was a show called Mystery Science Theater 2000, which ran bad Japanese sci-fi movie and had little cartoon figures heads in theater seats talking over the movie. If you ask me, the chatter of these little figures was more interesting than the film itself. Wanting to create the real-life version of that, we found Tim Conway Jr. and some of his friends to be the group that people could join and watch the shows with. It even got to the point where they would be watching a show and then decide it was boring and instruct the audience to turn to a different channel. That must have drove the Nielsen audience measurement crazy.

Without a doubt, we were onto something, and it was working. However, it all came to a screeching halt when the Microsoft guy in charge got very defensive, believing that we were showing him up. He made up some story about us misusing MS IP and called the Microsoft police to escort us out of the studio building. Despite that, we still continued to work with the other parts of Microsoft. And as a bonus, we understood this less-than-genius person got fired not long after.

While I was brought in as a consultant because I had no other corporate agenda or bias, I ended my two-year relationship as Microsoft's primary consultant to Interactive TV strategy because I didn't want to be beholden to their agenda.

We went on from there to serve in a similar capacity to one of Paul Allen's companies, called Digeo. Many of the creative concepts we developed in both places are in play today as the technology that allows us to do so many of the things we can do today that we never even thought about before. When the US moved to digital TV and the Internet got fast enough to support high quality video, so many new things became possible.

And I have to give credit where credit is due. A great deal of what we developed was in conjunction with Rick Portin. We were good at coming up with the creative ideas, but Rick knew how to harness the right technology and implement them. He was instrumental in taking us from idea to application and bringing our new technologies to the public.

17 No, I'M NOT GAY...
BUT MANY OF MY FRIENDS ARE

I am not gay (not that there is anything wrong with that), but some of my dearest and closest friends are. And as associations often do, because I hang out with them, there are some who assume that I am gay, too.

A few years ago, I was contacted by a creative branding guy in the fashion industry by the name of Darren Mayer, who asked me to work with him on an original TV concept, taking ESPORTS stars and mixing them with famous celebrities and then having them compete on a TV series. To put it into context, it was a bit like the old ABC show, Battle of the Network Stars. We worked on that development, and I had high hopes for it, but it seems Darren, who now was going by the name Mr. D, already had another big idea. He wanted to build a social media site that was a communications and connection vehicle for the LBGQI community. It was called BTYKWEEN (pronounce beauty queen) and was, indeed, potentially even bigger than the idea he proposed to me, and I became an advisor. He brought in iconic fashion designer Richie Rich to help connect them to a legion of folks from that community to be brand ambassadors and content creators. When the press got wind of this, they published a picture of Mr. D, Richie Rich and me. Now Mr. D wasn't quite sure which side of the fence he was playing on, but he dressed in his unique style, which led most people to assume that he was part of that community. To his credit, Richie was an inspiration to many young folks who still credit him with giving them the courage to come out. So when people saw the photos of me with them, it stirred speculation, and I got loads of emails and social media comments saying, "Oh, it's about time you came out. You like fashion, cooking, and showtunes, so we always thought you were but now we know."

Rather than trying to clarify (I'm about as hetero as they come), I just went with it and even let Rich and D influence my way of dressing. I started to pay attention to what I wore and upgraded my look. I even wear crocs as my daily footwear.

Now, there isn't anything wrong with being gay, but I found that there were some drawbacks. The only time I was ever told I couldn't go into a restaurant in LA was when we were all going to Mastro's in Beverly Hills, and the security guy at the door wouldn't let us in because of what D was wearing. I think it was women's Prada pants and sandals. No big deal—we went to the Palm, instead. They let us in.

Now, while this project was moving along nicely (everyone thought it was a genius idea), Mr. D met a girl. I guess he decided which team he was going to play on because he distanced himself from the BTYKWEEN team and was particularly nasty to Richie Rich. He was new at management and tried to get Richie to do morning reports and memos. When I learned this, I tried to explain that Richie is a pure creative and not a corporate soldier, but that didn't sink in. I even offered to manage the creative folks until the company could hire someone to assume that role, but that was also ignored, and the situation just kept getting worse. Rather than let me manage Richie and Kevin Aviance, a 7-foot-tall androgynous drag persona, who was and is still a very popular DJ in NYC, D distanced not only distanced himself from me and Kevin, but he also fired Richie. That was it for me. It was simply too much drama, and I wasn't going to compete with the girlfriend when it came to guiding D.

Soon after, we heard that the girlfriend was made an executive of the company and was listed as being a founder. As far as we knew, though, she was a real estate person in Beverly Hills and had no experience with anything that could justify any of these moves. We all predicted that the romance would come to a screeching halt at some point, and we were right in that assumption. She dumped him, which was sad, because by doing so, he lost his girlfriend, his company, and more important, his friends. On a side note, it was right after this that Richie changed his moniker to "Mr. C."

Thankfully, Richie recovered quickly—actually, it was a blessing in disguise because it enabled him to get back to his roots as a fashion designer. His previous brand was called Heatherette and was worn by folks like Madonna, Lady Gaga, Katy Perry, Paris Hilton, Pam Anderson, and many more. Richie even reached national recognition for designing the famous "Carrie" t-shirt that was worn on Sex and the City. Kudos to Patricia Fields for recognizing Richie's talents early on. Richie's brand was a success, and he sold it to Damon John of Shark Tank fame.

Just about a year ago, Richie decided to jump back in with a new brand, which he named Richererette. That brand is in its early stages, and 2025 is slated to be its breakout year. While he is readying runway shows for NY and LA fashion weeks in the fall, I am an advisor to him and Cicero Oca (the person who really keeps Richie organized and on schedule), and I have an equity stake in the company.

What is a Richie Rich fashion show like? I describe it as a circus on steroids. It is so unconventional and just as much fun. He doesn't use the standard models but instead insists on using everyday people of all colors, shapes, and sizes. For example, his last show featured an elderly woman in a wheelchair, a skateboarder smoking a cigarette, skinny guys in thongs, and the list goes on. My son, Jon, even walked in his runway shows. Next, my new grandson, Bodin, will unveil a new part of the line called Baby Richerette. At the tender age of one year, he's landed his first modeling gig—nepotism at its finest.

The connection between me and Richie is odd since he was a NYC nightlife fixture and part of what was called "The Club Kids," who controlled the entrance to most of the hot clubs in LA. I always looked too straight and never would get in. While Richie wasn't the one at the door turning me away, I still give him shit about it. The Club Kids were well known for a while, but they came to an abrupt, unexpected end when one of the most visible members was involved in a murder.

Regardless of the fact that I'm straight, I'm a firm believer that everyone has the right to find their own happiness and path in life, and as long as they are not hurting anyone, anything, or the planet, we should not get in the way of their search for happiness. That goes for more than one's sexuality—I have even come to terms with and become accepting of vegans.

Some of my most fun times are when Richie and his crew come over for dinner. My kids love them all, and it gives me pleasure to know that I managed to raise some thoughtful and kind kids. One of my greatest memories is when we went to a Dodgers game together and discovered that Richie knows as much about baseball as we do. It turns out that his dad was a sports editor for the NY Times and always supported him. Instead of shunning Richie, who knew he was different even from a very young age, his parents accepted and nurtured him. It just shows how good and loving parenting can turn out wonderful human beings of all persuasions. Richie's mom passed away last year, and I can vouch for the fact that they were extremely close until the very end.

I feel the same. Richie will remain my friend, regardless if our friendship leads people to believe that I am gay. I am not, but many of my friends are, and I'm proud to say that Richie is one of them.

CHAPTER 18

THE THINGS THAT CHANGED ME

Naturally, my childhood and my family had a huge impact on who I am and what I believe. As a child of immigrant parents, I grew up with a love for America that hasn't wavered; however, the Vietnam War taught me that I don't have to agree with our politicians or government to be patriotic. After losing people I cared about in that war and having heartfelt discussions with other people who were personally impacted by the loss of their loved ones, I realized that I can be patriotic and still have my own opinion, even if it isn't a popular one. Even more, we can still be friends, despite our differences. We may not agree on everything, but we can always respect each other's right to have a different opinion.

Talking about differences, I grew up in a poor neighborhood in Coney Island, though I didn't know it at the time. After graduating from college with a career as a teacher on the horizon, the trajectory of my life changed when New York issued a five-year moratorium on hiring teachers. Little did I know at the time, that moratorium opened the door to a career and a life that was beyond my imagination—one where a lowly assistant cable splice cutter would climb the ladder and eventually found his own entertainment network and be instrumental in bringing the media and entertainment industry to Russia and China.

Imagine what it was like for me, the child of lower-class immigrants who was working in the underground bowels of the Big Apple, to find himself swimming in a piano-shaped pool in a lavish mansion in LA. Talk about a life-changing and eye-opening move! Never in my wildest dreams did I imagine that I would wine and dine with Hollywood elites and celebrities.

E! was such a huge success, and Alan and I were lauded as geniuses. Publicity was everywhere, and we were getting invited to exclusive Hollywood events. Let me tell you, it was really easy to get caught up in all the laudatory bullshit that comes with stardom. Then I got involved in what I thought would be even bigger than E!. In my eyes, it was a sure thing. At the time, the Internet was taking off and domain names were going for big bucks. We partnered with a guy who owned several major domain names, including TELEVISION.com. We were offered big money for it but turned it down and launched it ourselves. However, the technology wasn't ready to support what we wanted to do, and then the Internet economy crashed. We lost our butts on that one.

But I learned something that has benefitted me from that day forward. I learned that I need to reassess all the things I'm planning every night and pay attention to the environments we operate in. And I discovered that the ideas I had in the morning were usually not so good that night. It was a life lesson that I'll never forget and one that I hope can save others from jumping too fast without doing their homework. There is nothing wrong with admitting you are not so smart that you can't sometimes be wrong. Everything you come up with is not always golden. Be honest with yourself and put your ego aside. Then, when a great idea comes, you'll be better prepared and know if you really should act on it—or put it on backburner, at least for now.

There are so many things and people who have changed my life. Learning about different cultures and living in different countries is at the top of the list. Surprisingly, my childhood and upbringing prepared me for that. Growing up in a mixed, diverse neighborhood helped to shape my feelings toward learning other cultures and become comfortable in other countries. My parents taught me to have respect when visiting someone else's home. My mother would always say, "If you don't like their rules, then you should go elsewhere." That stuck with me throughout my life, and it had a big impact on how I managed to navigate Russia and China. After all, I was an American, but I was in their house and had to respect their rules. Because of this, I was able to form lasting relationships with many of the people I met during my international endeavors—and I likely kept my butt out of trouble during the reign of the Soviet Union and my encounter with the turf "bosses."

While I can laugh about that experience now, there are some experiences that were so serious and life changing that they have forever left a mark on my heart. Not surprising, those experiences involve the people I love—my family, my children, and my grandchild.

It would be impossible for me to write any book, even one highlighting my career, without mentioning my family. I am, above all, a proud father and grandfather, and my family means everything to me. Being their dad means the world to me, and I don't want to know what it would be like without them in my lives.

Unfortunately, there was a time when the wellbeing and life of one of my children was at stake. I was divorced at the time, and my ex-wife, Carolyn, called me, concerned that our 15-year-old son, Jon, might be drinking or doing drugs. When I asked why she would think that, she explained that she had watched him trying to do his homework and noticed that he couldn't put his pencil on the line. My first thought was that he might need glasses, so I suggested she take him to the eye doctor to get his eyes checked. That was more believable than the possibility that he was doing anything wrong. To be honest, if she had said that our daughter was drinking or doing drugs, I might have bought it. But not Jon. No, Jon was too much like his mom, who had attended Catholic schools for 12 years and never told a lie.

Carolyn did take him to the eye doctor, and Jon did need glasses. We thought that was the end of that, but she called me a week later and said the glasses hadn't taken care of the problem, so she was taking Jon back to the eye doctor. This time, they said he had a muscle disorder in his eye and needed minor surgery to fix it. Carolyn trusted her instincts and didn't blindly accept this diagnosis, and she demanded they schedule Jon for further testing. The eye doctor objected, saying he knew what he was doing and she shouldn't put Jon through all of that for no reason. She insisted, not taking no for an answer, and he acquiesced.

Then I got the call no parent wants to get. Carolyn was right—there was much more wrong than an eye problem or a muscle disorder. Jon had cancer, specifically, he had a rare brain tumor that typically is only seen in boys going through puberty. We had to see a brain cancer doctor right away, as it was apparent that he was literally getting worse by the day. His speech had become slurred. and he started repeating himself over and over. We were lucky and got in to see the doctor that afternoon, and he was very honest about what was going on. He came right out and told us that this was a rare form of cancer, and generally these kids aren't diagnosed until an autopsy is performed. Usually, they are mistakenly diagnosed with—you guessed it—a muscle disorder of the eye. The tumor grows over a vital duct in the brain, and the person dies of brain failure before cancer.

Being 15, Jon was aware of his diagnosis. His take on all this was that he needed to be cured quickly so he wouldn't miss Lacrosse practice. Naturally, we wanted him to be treated quickly because we wanted to do everything possible to save his life. He had experimental surgery, then chemotherapy, and then radiation. The treatment was aggressive, which was a good thing, because so was the cancer.

I am happy—no, ecstatic—to say that Jon recently celebrated his 20-year anniversary being cancer free. I know that cancer, his fight, and his survival changed him, and I can honestly say that it changed my life, perhaps more than anything I've ever undergone or experienced. There is nothing more important than family and friends, and experiences like this make you more aware of that. I've learned not to take my family or friends for granted—life is too short and far too fragile not to appreciate every day we have with the people we love. While there are so many things—from Coney Island, to LA, to Russia and China and beyond—that have changed me, the possibility of losing a child tops the list. With it, though, came a lesson that I will always hold close to my heart: I will cherish my children and loved ones while I can. I don't know what tomorrow will bring, but I will do everything I can to make sure I have no regrets today.

And I don't. I don't regret going to college to be a teacher, just as I don't regret taking a job as an assistant underground cable splicer. I don't regret moving to LA or the remarkable, memorable, and even controversial people and experiences that came into my life because of #E! Did I make mistakes? Sure, I did, but I don't have any regrets, for every person, every experience, and every undertaking became a part of who I am. And I will always be grateful for that.

CHAPTER 19

THE LARRY NAMER
RECIPE FOR SUCCESS

This book has featured the highlights of my journey. It's not a play-by-play of my life or career, and it's not meant to be. I never set out to write a tell-all book that would divulge all of my relationships or experiences, and I certainly didn't want to use this book as a tabloid to expose anyone else's scandals or secrets. If they want to reveal anything to the world, I'm sure they can, and will, write their own book.

I chose to share the stories in this book because they were influential, even pivotal, in my life. They told the story of how a poor kid from Coney Island found himself in the unlikeliest of places, living and working among the stars and the rich and famous in the entertainment capital of the world, Los Angeles.

In some ways, my story is unbelievable. Sometimes, I can't even believe it. But it's true. And that's what makes it remarkable. I mean, who would think that Alan and I, as naïve and inexperienced as we were, could actually create an entertainment channel that would change the entertainment industry? Looking back, I can see that the only reason we got any funding and succeeded was because we were inexperienced and didn't realize just how unlikely it was that anyone would take us seriously. In other words, we didn't know not to listen when we were told no. Ironically, that worked for us.

I credit our inexperience and naivety with our success. Without it, we would have thrown in the towel and given up and gone home.

Looking back, though, I realize that my success was due to multiple things, many that I learned from tried-and-true experience, and some that I was fortunate to learn from people who have been instrumental in my life. So, without further ado, I share with you the pivotal things I've learned and still live by.

Larry Namer's Recipe for Success:

- **When managing people, be firm but fair**. You can be as tough as the situation calls for, but be sure everyone around, above, and below understands and believes that your decisions are fair. I learned this from Nick Nicholas, who at the time was the President of Manhattan Cable and went on to be President of Time Warner. I have tried to stay true to this principle throughout my career and in everything I do, and I can attest to the fact that it is some of the best advice I have ever received. Thank you, Nick!

- **Don't let yesterday take up too much of today**. Or as Barry Diller said when his long-running attempt to take over Paramount failed, "NEXT!" Whatever happened yesterday cannot be undone, but what's done is done. Move on. Tomorrow is another day.

- **When doing business in Los Angeles, assume everyone is lying until they prove to you they are not.** LA is a very strange place that attracts all sorts of character from all over the world. It is really one of the very few BIG cities dominated by a single industry—entertainment. If I would tell someone I was doing a film deal in China, they would tell me they have a slate of films going. If I said I started a TV network, they would say they did, too (when all they really had was a website with a video window). After getting burned a few dozen times, I learned and adopted the mantra that they were all lying in their teeth—until they could prove to me otherwise.

- **You can't turn a tiger into a vegetarian, and a leopard doesn't change its spots**. Once you determine someone is dishonest, don't ever get fooled into thinking they will be a good partner for you. When someone shows you who they are, believe them. It's just a matter of time before they'll turn on you.

- **In a foreign country, respect their culture and their ways**. It's not up to you to change the way they live or what they value. You are a guest in their country and need to respect their culture, their lifestyle, their rules, and their laws. I learned that from my mom, and it proved to be invaluable. Because of her advice, the years I spent in Russia and China were successful, and I'm proud to say that because of her words, I enjoyed many mutually respectful relationships with people in different countries. Some are still good friends to this day.

- **Technology can't be held back and will always march on.** I learned this while being the primary consultant to Microsoft for interactive TV strategy. Take my word for it, it's true.

- **You can't out train a bad diet**. I wish I had accepted this principle earlier in life, but I'm thankful that I've embraced it now. As they say, hindsight is 20/20. I'm in the gym six days a week for an hour each time, but after years of eating anything I wanted, I now actually pay attention to what I'm eating and make an attempt to eat healthier. What turned the tables? I saw a picture of Alan, my E! partner, who was in intensive care from COVID. Believe me, that'll do it. Seeing someone you care about fighting for their life is life changing. It changed me. I decided right then and there to get healthy, and I dropped over 50 pounds. I admit that I still love food—that hasn't changed—but I now limit my not-so-healthy meals to once a day and make sure that the others are healthy.

- **The most important thing in life is to be happy.** I'm not sure where I got this one, but I stand by it 1,000 percent. My mom used to be worried about my daughter, and she'd often ask, "Are Nicole and her boyfriend serious and planning to get married?" I would say that I didn't care if they got married as long as she was happy. Married or not, her happiness was what really mattered. And I can apply this principle to anything in life, and it still holds water. Do what makes you happy. You don't have to answer to anyone but yourself.

- **The future belongs to those who prepare for it today** - Malcolm X. The years I spent envisioning the different ways cable could be used prove this to be true. Tomorrow will come. Look ahead. Prepare for it. Heck, be a part of it and participate in creating it. If you don't, life will pass you by, and you'll find yourself wondering why you were left behind.

- **Let yourself be who you really are.** Fashion designer Richie Rich, who is an icon in the LGBTQ+ community and has dressed everyone from Madonna to Lady Gaga, taught me this. He even made me a sweatshirt with this saying on it. And he's right. I never tried to be some high-profile executive or a mogul in the entertainment industry. That's not who I am. I'm just Larry Namer, a guy from Coney Island who happened to get some lucky breaks and take some risks when I was too ignorant to know that the odds were against me. In LA, it's easy to forget where you came from, and I'm grateful for friends like Richie who love me just the way I am.

- **Don't take yourself too seriously**. This came from Haile Bailey. And I'm proud to say that I don't. I still see myself as just another schmuck from Brooklyn. To this day, I'm constantly astounded by people who show such reverence for the Founder of E!. Honestly, I see myself as a regular guy who got lucky. Sure, I'm grateful, but in my opinion, I'm not all that.

- **Following your passion is a road to starving.** Now, there might be some folks who will beg to differ with that statement, so let me explain. Anyone who follows me on social media knows I'm a food nut. I love to cook—I mean I really love to cook, and I love to eat. To say I'm passionate about food would be an understatement. If there was one thing that I really wanted to do, I would have owned a restaurant and been a chef. I love cooking that much. So, of course, I invested in some restaurant deals throughout the years. Spoiler alert: I lost money every time. It turns out that I'm not good at two things: making movies and owning restaurants. From experience, I've learned that following my passion is a fast path to homelessness. The best recipe for success is to pick something you are really good at and invest yourself in that. You will get better at it, and in time you will become passionate about it. My story is the perfect example.

This brings me to this book. Over the years, people who have heard the story of my career have told me that I need to write a book, a suggestion that I've always shut down. I'm still a simple guy from Coney Island, and I never needed that feather in my cap. Besides, while I knew my story was somewhat unique, I didn't feel compelled to share it with the world.

But then it occurred to me that there is one thing that I love sharing—my cooking. My love for cooking began when I was a latchkey kid who got tired of eating peanut butter and jelly sandwiches when my parents were at work. Out of necessity, I learned how to make recipes I found in my mom's cookbooks. And then I started creating my own recipes. I got so good at it that I was able to taste a dish and go home and recreate it in my own kitchen.

And I loved every minute of it. Even more, I love sharing the food I cook with my family and friends. In fact, there are few things that make me happier. And this brings me to why I wrote this book. It occurred to me that if I wrote a book, it would be a way for me to share my true passion with everyone. After all, I can't possibly cook for everyone … but, hey, I can still share what I cook with everyone. Realizing that a book was a way to share my love of cooking, the idea grew on me. It was genius, really—writing a cookbook disguised as a memoir isn't something just anybody can pull off, but I'm Larry Namer, the guy who has a track record for doing what others have said couldn't (or shouldn't) be done.

The first part of this book featured my background and some of the pivotal, colorful, and, yes, humorous highlights of my life and career. It is off script—a behind-the-scenes take on my life and career, and it is unapologetically and authentically me. In the next section, I share with you my true passion—the recipes I've created and served to my friends and loved ones throughout the years. They, too, are authentic, and every one of them has earned the nod of approval from myself (my biggest food critic) and my guests. I hope you enjoy them as much as I've enjoyed creating and perfecting them.

I'm Larry Namer, and my life has always been off script—and if you ask me, that's a pretty good place to be. It's also the main ingredient in my recipe for success. It's what happened behind the scenes that changed the trajectory of my life. I wouldn't have it any other way.

My Dad

Dad's Mom

Me and Dad when I was cute

Me and Stan Rogow in 7th grade.
Stan became Disney Channel's top producer of Lizzie Maguire,
among many others

NAMER, LARRY

High school football

My mom and Nicole

The network before we changed the name to E!

Here I am in a tux and bow tie getting honored with the President's Award from the National Cable TV Association. Also pictured: Ted Turner, Geraldine Laybourne (started Nickelodeon), Kay Koplovitz (started USA and Sci-Fi networks), John Hendricks (started Discovery), and Bob Johnson (started BET). I guess it was a very good year for innovation. (I'm the youngest in the group.)

With Tony Bennett

Me and supermodel Claudia Schiffer

With Manny Pacquiao, Boxing Champ

Me and Vladimir Putin, back when hair was in

With China's top film and TV star, Yang Mi

With famous Korean actress, Clara Lee

On the set of Return to Da Fu Tsun

Our China Company

Our first show in China: Hello Hollywood

With China's Oprah, Yu Sai Kan

On the red carpet at the Shanghai Film Festival

I'm cooking Sichuan chicken dish for my show on Beijing TV

With Frank Shankwitz,
Cofounder of Make a Wish Foundation

David Koz and I at Secret Knock 2024

With Richie Rich and Friends

My grandson, Bodin

My sons, Jon and Alexander

Getting 2024 Media Visionary Award from astronaut
Bruce Melnick at the Kennedy Space Center

The recipient of the Hollywood Lifetime Achievement
in Entertainment Award:
Producer Larry Namer

SECTION TWO

LARRY NAMER'S
RECIPES

I taught myself how to cook when I was growing up.
I hope you enjoy some of these recipes as much as I did and still do!
Let's get started with some baked clams…

Baked Clams

BAKED CLAMS

Ingredients

3 Tbsp butter
3 Tbsp extra virgin olive oil
1 small diced onion
3 cloves minced garlic
1 Tbsp Old Bay seasoning
1 Tbsp fresh squeezed lemon juice
1 tsp dried oregano
1 tsp chopped fresh basil
1 jar of clam juice
2 dozen cherrystone clams (if you can't find fresh, get 3 cans)
1 tsp chopped parsley
2 tsp grated parmesan cheese
1 pound box of thin spaghetti or linguini
Pinch of crushed dried red pepper flakes
Pinch of salt
1/2 tsp cornstarch

In a large skillet, sauté olive oil, garlic, and onion.

At the same time, put the clams in a steamer until they open, then cool them down with cold water and remove the clams from the shells and set aside. Reserve the water from the steamer.

Start boiling the water for the spaghetti with a pinch of salt added to the water.

Add the clams and the jar of clam juice to the skillet. Add the lemon juice and Old Bay.

When the pasta is cooked (al dente), remove it with a slotted spoon or pasta fork and add it to the skillet.

Add the crushed pepper and parmesan cheese.

Mix 1/4 cup of the clam juice from the steamer with the cornstarch and add to the skillet. Raise the heat until the sauce thickens. Then shut the flame.

Plate the pasta, sauce, and clams and garnish with parsley and chopped basil. If sauce is too thick, use some of the water from the steamer to thin it. Serve with garlic bread.

CHICKEN PARMIGIANA

Ingredients:

Sauce:

- 1 tsp garlic, minced
- 2 cans tomato sauce
- 1 tsp dried oregano
- 1 tsp sugar
- 1 tsp crushed black pepper
- 1 tsp salt
- 4 Tbsp red wine

Chicken:

- 2 chicken breasts, sliced to make them thinner or buy already thin
- 2 beaten eggs
- 2 cups Italian bread crumbs
- 1 cup all-purpose flour
- 1 cup olive oil
- Pinch of salt
- 4 oz of grated parmesan cheese
- 12 oz of sliced mozzarella

Prepare the sauce by frying some minced garlic in olive oil, then add two cans of tomato sauce. Add 1 tsp of dried oregano, 1 tsp sugar, 1 tsp crushed black pepper, 4 Tbsp red wine, 1 tsp salt. Cook over low heat for 30 minutes.

Slice chicken breast in half in such a way that they are thinner, not smaller. Place one at a time on a cutting board and cover with a sheet of wax paper. With the flat side of a meat cleaver, pound them until very thin. Coat each one with all-purpose flour. Then dip in egg wash until totally coated, then coat with Italian bread crumbs. Press them firmly into the bread crumbs so they stick and cover entirely.

In a frying pan, heat 4 Tbsp of olive oil and fry the chicken cutlets until they turn lightly brown on each side. Flip them as they brown. Remove from the frying pan and dry on paper towels.

Coat the bottom of an oven tray with a bit of the sauce, then place the fried chicken breasts so they lay flat. Cover with the rest of the sauce, then sprinkle with grated parmesan cheese. Place the sliced mozzarella cheese on top. Preheat oven to 350 degrees. Place the pan in the oven and cook for 45 minutes. Remove and serve (generally with a pasta that is not with red sauce).

Pairs well with a plain salad topped with a simple vinaigrette dressing—and, of course, a bottle of red wine.

BURRATA AND TOMATO

Ingredients

2 balls of fresh burrata, each cut in half to make 4 servings
1 large heirloom tomato sliced into 4 pieces
1 bunch arugula
4 Tbsp virgin olive oil
2 Tbsp balsamic vinegar
1 squirt balsamic vinegar crema
4 leaves fresh basil chopped
Pinch salt
Pinch white pepper

In a salad bowl, mix the arugula with the olive oil, balsamic vinegar, salt and pepper. Then divide it and place on plates. Add 1 tomato slice to each. Drizzle the balsamic crema over the cheese and around the plate. Sprinkle with chopped basil and serve.

SWEET AND SOUR CHICKEN

Ingredients

1 pound of boneless, skinless chicken thighs cut into 1-inch cubes
Kosher salt (2 pinches)
White pepper (pinch)
3 Tbsp light soy sauce
3 Tbsp all-purpose flour
1 Tbsp cornstarch
1 cup chicken stock
2 Tbsp ketchup
2 Tbsp brown sugar
2 Tbsp white vinegar
2 cups avocado oil
1 medium onion, sliced
1 8-oz can pineapple chunks
1 egg
1 red pepper cut into 1-inch slices
1 green pepper cut into 1-inch slices

To prepare the chicken, first marinate it for at least 1 hour by placing the pieces into a 1-gallon freezer bag with the soy sauce, 1 pinch of salt, white pepper, flour, and egg. Mix well to be sure all the chicken gets marinated.

In a bowl, prepare the sauce. It is important to have this ready in advance as the dish comes together quickly. Mix the chicken stock, ketchup, brown sugar, white vinegar, and cornstarch. Blend together until smooth.

Mix the chicken coating—the flour, cornstarch, salt, and baking powder—together a separate bowl. Dredge the chicken pieces, being careful to make sure each piece is coated. You can do that put pressing the dry coating onto the chicken with your hands.

In a pot, fry the chicken in the oil. The oil should be between 325 and 350 degrees before you add chicken pieces. When brown, remove them and put on a paper towel. When all the chicken is done, you will fry the pieces one more time until they are golden brown. Double cooking the chicken ensures they are crispy. Remove from the oil and set aside.

In a wok or deep frying pan, sauté the pepper and onions in a few tablespoons of the oil you just fried the chicken in. When cooked to being medium soft, add the chicken and sauté for another minute. Then pour in the sauce and cook until sauce thickens (about 2 minutes).

Serve this dish with a side of steamed rice.

CHINESE STYLE SPARE RIBS

I learned this one working in the kitchen of House of King,
an old-school Chinese restaurant in Brooklyn.

Ingredients

1 rack of St. Louis style cut ribs (divided into two even pieces)
1/4 cup soy sauce
1/4 cup hoisin sauce (just about every market has this now)
1/4 cup pineapple or orange juice
1 tsp of Chinese 5-spice powder
Pinch of white pepper
Pinch of garlic salt
1/4 cup brown sugar
2 Tbsp honey
1 Tbsp sesame oil
1 Tbsp red food coloring

Mix all the ingredients together and add to a gallon-size freezer bag. Add the two pieces of ribs. Marinate at least 4 hours. Preheat oven to 400 degrees. When up to temp, place ribs on the middle rack of the oven and roast for 35 minutes. Remove and let cool for 5 minutes. Slice into individual ribs and plate. Serve with Colemans English mustard and Golds Duck sauce.

Cooking became therapeutic for me throughout the years. Here is a little "therapy" from my years with Manhattan Cable, a favorite, Shrimp Egg Rolls.

New York Style Shrimp Egg Rolls

NEW YORK STYLE SHRIMP EGG ROLLS

Ingredients

1 package of egg roll wrappers (most supermarkets have these now)
1/2 pound cooked medium shrimp each cut into 4 pieces
1/4 head of napa cabbage
1 stalk celery, cut into very small pieces
1 handful of copped bean sprouts (fresh not canned)
1 Tbsp cornstarch
2 Tbsp light soy sauce
1 egg, whisked

For Cooking
4 cups vegetable oil

NOTE: For this recipe, buy the egg roll wrappers, as they are as good, if not better, than any you could make at home. Then you should watch a YouTube video on how to assemble the egg rolls as there is simply no way it will work if I tell you how in writing.

Mix all the filling ingredients together in a bowl. Lay out an egg roll wrapper and place two heaping spoonsful of the filling near the middle ... but a drop more to the part closest to you. Roll as you learned from the video. Dip your fingers into the whisked egg and seal. Then place another wrapper down and roll and seal. Having two wrappers is key to getting crispy egg rolls.

To cook, heat the oil and toss in a piece of leftover egg roll wrapper to make sure the oil is hot enough to fry them. Cook each egg roll until light brown, then remove and dry on a paper towel. When they are all halfway cooked, cook them in the hot oil until they are a nice golden brown. Remove and place on paper towels. Then cut each in half and place on a serving plate. Frying them twice is what gives them the absolute crispiness.

Serve with some homemade English mustard (make it from powder and let stand at least ten minutes). I use Colemans. Also, serve with store-bought duck sauce for dipping.

Gazpacho

GAZPACHO

Ingredients for the base

1 14-oz can peeled tomatoes
1 small can tomato juice
1 Tbsp red wine vinegar
1 Persian cucumber, peeled and chopped
1 garlic clove, diced
2 red bell peppers (remove seeds and roughly chop)
1 red chili pepper (remove seeds and roughly chop)
1 small yellow onion (diced)
1/4 cup olive oil
Pinch sea salt
Pinch ground black pepper
Tabasco to taste

Croutons (I found the packaged ones work well)
Small package of Caesar-flavored croutons

The finishing ingredients

Fresh tomato, seeded and chopped
Persian cucumber diced into ¼ inch pieces
1 red chili, seeded and diced
1 green bell pepper, seeded and diced

Place all the base ingredients into a blender and blend well. Put in a bowl and refrigerate overnight.

When ready to serve, prepare the finishing ingredients. In each bowl, ladle some of the base and top with finishing ingredients and croutons

PEPPERS AND ANCHOVIES

Ingredients

I can flat anchovies
5 red peppers
4 Tbsp olive oil
Pinch of salt
Pinch of black pepper
1 tsp dried oregano
1/4 cup chopped parsley
1/2 cup red wine vinegar
1/4 cup olive oil

On the stove, char the red peppers until they are blackened on all sides. Put in a paper bag and let steam. Then peel and seed them. Cut into 2-inch slices and put in a jar with the vinegar, salt, pepper, oregano. Refrigerate and leave overnight.

When ready to serve add peppers to each plate. Sprinkle with the olive oil and garnish with parsley. Put an anchovy on each piece of pepper.

*I was with Valley Cable and living In Los Angeles when I had La Scala Salad.
I remember it well—Alan and I were having lunch with OJ Simpson, who had
a score to settle. I liked the salad so much I replicated it at home.*

La Scala Chopped Salad

LA SCALA CHOPPED SALAD

Ingredients

Dressing:

1/3 cup extra virgin olive oil
3 Tbsp red wine vinegar
1minced garlic clove
3 Tbsp Dijon mustard
1/4 tsp kosher salt
1/4 tsp fine ground black pepper
1/4 cup grated Pecorino Romano cheese

Salad:

1 head shredded iceberg lettuce (5-6 cups)
1 small head of romaine lettuce shredded
14 oz can of chickpeas, drained and rinsed
1/4 pound of genoa salami thinly sliced
2 cups shredded mozzarella cheese

Wisk together all the dressing ingredients

In a large bowl mix the salad ingredients and then pour dressing over and mix. Plate the salad into individual portions.

CHINESE CUCUMBER SALAD

Ingredients

4 Persian cucumbers cut into 1/2-inch rounds
4 Tbsp soy sauce
4 Tbsp sesame oil
4 Tbsp rice wine vinegar
4 Tbsp Mirin
1 tsp salt
Pinch of white pepper (or if you like spicy and can find Sichuan Pepper)
White sesame seeds

In a bowl, mix all the liquid ingredients.

Put the cucumber slices in a Mason jar; pour the liquid mix into jar.

Cover and refrigerate for 1-2 hours.

In the service bowl, put the cucumber in the liquid and sprinkle with sesame seeds.

Borshct

BORSHCT

Jewish-style served cold with no meat added

Ingredients

2 Tbsp vegetable oil
8 cups vegetable stock
1 pound beets, peeled and coarsely grated
1 small can diced tomato
2 medium carrots, peeled and cut into ¼ inch pieces
3 garlic cloves, diced
2 medium Yukon gold potatoes, diced into ¼ inch pieces
1/2 small head of cabbage chopped
1/4 cup chopped parsley
Dill to garnish

Put vegetable oil into a pot and start to cook. Add the beets, carrots, garlic, and potato and cook for about 6 minutes, constantly stirring. Add the vegetable stock and the diced tomatoes. Cook for another 6 minutes over medium heat. Add the cabbage and cook another 2 minutes. Let this cool, add the parsley, then put in fridge for at least 3 hours. Serve in bowls topped with a dollop of sour cream and garnished with dill.

I cooked Sichuan Chicken in an episode of my cooking show in Beijing, China. I hope you enjoy it.

Sichuan Chicken

SICHUAN CHICKEN

Ingredients

For the marinade:
Pinch white pepper
1/4 cup rice wine
1/4 cup dark soy sauce
1/4 cup light soy sauce
1 Tbsp corn flour
4 boneless/skinless chicken thighs

For the cooked chicken:
Pinch of white pepper
Crushed Sichuan peppercorns (you might need to get from an Asian store)
1/4 cup light soy sauce
2 cloves crushed garlic
1 tsp sugar, peppercorns
1 Tbsp minced ginger
1 Tbsp ketchup
1/4 cup peanut oil
1 red chili pepper, finely diced
1 spring onion chopped (white and green parts)

Cut the chicken into 1-inch pieces and place in a freezer bag. Add the rest of the marinate ingredients, seal the bag, and marinate for at least 2 hours or overnight in fridge.

Heat the peanut oil in a wok or big frying pan. When visibly hot, remove from the bag and fry them until they are golden. Remove from the pan and dry on a paper towel. Add the diced chili and fry for 1 minute. Then add the ginger, sugar, garlic, peppercorns, and fry for another minute. Then add the soy sauce and ketchup and stir. Add back the cooked chicken for another minute. Remove and plate, sprinkling on the green onion.

Serve over steamed rice.

MISO COD WITH PEAS AND MUSHROOMS

Ingredients
4 oz of cod per person individual portions
4 oz of sake
2 oz of soy sauce
2 oz of Mirin (sweet wine)
2 Tbsp of brown sugar

For the sauce:
1/2 cup heavy cream
1/2 cup frozen peas
2 sliced shitake mushrooms
Pinch of salt
Pinch of pepper
Very small pinch of nutmeg
1 tsp cornstarch
1/2 cup chicken stock

Marinate the cod in the fridge for 2-3 days.

Remove from the bag and place it on a broiler pan and let come to room temp (about 20 minutes).

In a saucepan, sauté the mushrooms for 2 minutes, then add the peas and the stock. Cook for 2 more minutes.

Add the cornstarch to the heavy cream and mix well. Add to the saucepan and stir until the sauce thickens a bit. Salt and pepper to taste and add the pinch of nutmeg.

Broil (middle rack) the cod for about 8 minutes—it should be a caramelized brown when ready.

Ladle some of the sauce into individual bowls, then place a piece of the cod in each. Serve with Italian bread to sop up the sauce.

Goes well with a plain salad with vinaigrette dressing.

MATZO BALL SOUP

Ingredients

For the soup:
    3 14-oz chicken broth
    4 chicken thighs
    2 carrots
    1 stalk celery
    1 small onion
    1 parsnip
    1 pinch pepper

For the matzo balls:
    2 cups matzo meal
    1/4 cup melted chicken fat (or any neutral oil)
    2 Tbsp minced dill
    1 Tbsp minced parsley
    1 Tbsp minced tarragon
    6 beaten eggs
    1/2 cup seltzer
    Pinch of salt

In a bowl, combine the matzo meal, fat, herbs, salt, and eggs and mix until smooth. Add the seltzer and mix again. Refrigerate for 2 hours.

While the matzo ball mix is in the fridge, prepare the soup. Add chicken broth and I quart of water to a large pot and boil. Lower flame and add chicken thighs and cook over low heat for 3 hours. At the 2-hour point, and celery, carrot, and parsnip that has been cut into 2-inch pieces. Add a pinch of pepper.

After two hours, form the matzo ball mixture into small balls and add to boiling salted water. Cook for about 45-50 minutes until they expand and fill the pot.

To serve, add a matzo ball to a bowl and ladle over the soup and a few vegetables. Sprinkle with a sprig of dill and serve.

FRIED RICE

NOTE: This dish works best with day old rice.
Freshly made rice will clump and be sticky.

Ingredients

3 cups day old jasmine rice
3 Tbsp peanut oil
½ pound protein, either shrimp, pork, chicken, or beef, chopped
2 beaten eggs
1 clove minced garlic
1 Tbsp minced ginger
2 Tbsp soy sauce
4 green onions sliced into 1/8 inch pieces

Heat the oil in a wok or large skillet. Stir in the protein and cook until done. Remove from the wok, but leave the oil. Add the eggs and stir until they set. Remove ad reserve.

Add the ginger and garlic. Cook for 1 minute. Add the rice and stir that for about 3 minutes. Add the soy sauce and stir so it distributes evenly and colors the rice. Add back the protein and the egg. Stir. Shut the flame and add the green onions. Serve.

AVOCADO AND RED ONION SALAD

Ingredients
1 small red onion, peeled and sliced into 1/8-inch slices
2 Tbsp sugar
2 ripe avocados, peeled, halved, and cut into 1/2-inch slices

For the dressing:
1/3 cup virgin olive oil
1/4 cup balsamic vinegar
Pinch sea salt
Pinch white pepper

In a small bowl, put 1 cup of water and add the sugar. Mix until dissolved. Add the onion and let stand for at least one hour. This will make the onion taste much milder.

After an hour or two, remove the onion and dry in a paper towel. Set aside.

Don't slice the avocado until you are close to serving or it will discolor.

After slicing, put on flat plates and spread the onions on top of each.

While the onions are soaking, make the dressing by combining 1/3 cup of virgin olive oil with 1/4 cup balsamic vinegar, a pinch of sea salt, and a pinch of white pepper. Wisk vigorously, then drizzle over the avocado and onion mixture.

BAKED CLAMS OREGANATA

The family would eat out every Sunday night, and Italian was a once-a-month event. The go-to restaurant was Carolinas, which is no longer a fixture in Coney Islan Brooklyn. They had the best baked clams, and over the years, I have tried to replicate that dish. This came pretty close.

Ingredients for 2 people
> 1 dozen fresh little neck clams
> 1 cup Italian bread crumbs
> 1 lemon
> Extra virgin olive oil
> Chopped garlic
> Fresh parsley
> Grated parmesan cheese
> Salt
> Black pepper
> Red pepper flakes (optional)
> 1/2 cup white wine
> I bottle clam juice

Clean the clams by running under cold water and removing any grit.

Add 1 cup of water to a saucepan and add the clams. Turn on the flame and cover the pan. Cook until the clams open. Keep checking and remove the ones that open with tongs and immediately dip in cold water to stop the cooking. Remove them until they are all opened and out of the pan.

With a sharp knife, separate the clam from the muscle and snap off the half shell without the clam. Discard those. Save the clam broth that has been made from the water, plus the juice that came out of the clams.

In a bowl, mix the bread crumbs, chopped parsley, chopped garlic, salt, black pepper (red pepper also if you like it spicy), and two tablespoons of parmesan cheese. Add one-half cup of the freshly made clam juice to the mixture and one tablespoon of olive oil. Mix well.

With a teaspoon, add the mixture to the top of each clam in its shell. Sprinkle with a little more olive oil. In a baking pan, add the remaining fresh clam juice, the bottle of clam juice, and the white wine. Place the clams into the pan with half the liquid and then put into a preheated broiler until the topping browns. Remove and place on a deep serving platter. Add the liquid from the pan to the serving platter and add the lemon. which has been cut into quarters. Sprinkle a bit of the liquid over the top of the clams. Serve.

EGG FOO YUNG

Here's what I cooked this am when
I could not leave the house due to the LA fires.

Ingredients
   3 eggs
   1/2 red onion
   1/2 cup pork, shrimp, or chicken
   1 green onion, finely chopped
   1 pinch salt
   1 pinch pepper
   1 Tbsp Hoisin sauce
   1 Tbsp sesame oil
   1 Tbsp soy sauce
   1 Tbsp vegetable oil

Add two eggs to a bowl. Add just the yolk from the third egg. Whisk

In a small frying pan, add the oil and heat.

Add the onion and stir fry until soft.

Add cooked chicken, pork, or shrimp.

Add the beaten eggs and scramble with the onions.

In a small bowl, mix the remaining ingredients and prepare the sauce.

When eggs are set, remove to a plate and add sauce and green onion. Serve.

MY VERSION OF A WALDORF SALAD

Ingredients

- 3 celery stalks, finely chopped
- 4 heads of baby lettuce separated into the leaves
- 4 oz. of gruyere cheese, chopped coarsely
- 1/4 cup crushed almonds
- 3 red apples, sliced and peeled
- 2 radishes, thinly sliced

For the dressing:

- Juice of 1 meyer lemon
- 1 Tbsp white wine vinegar
- 5 Tbsp extra virgin olive oil
- 1/4 tsp Dijon mustard

Wisk the dressing ingredients together well.

Put the salad ingredients (minus the cheese) into a large salad bowl and season to taste with salt and pepper. Coat with the salad dressing, then plate it into individua portions. Sprinkle each with cheese and almonds. Serve.

SMASH BURGERS

Ingredients

For the burgers:
   1 pound 80% ground beef
   1/2 yellow onion, chopped fine
   1 egg
   Pinch salt
   Pinch black pepper
   1 package of potato hamburger buns
   Package of sliced gruyere cheese
   1 sliced tomato

For the sauce:
   1/2 cup ketchup
   2 Tbsp mayonnaise
   2 tsp relish
   1/2 Tbsp Dijon mustard

Make the burgers by mixing the ingredients together by hand (do not use a processor). Divide into 4 burgers. Preheat a cast iron skillet on the stove. When it's hot, cook the burgers for 3 minutes on each side. Toast the buns in the oven with a slice of cheese on each. Remove when the cheese is melted. Slather the buns with the sauce, then add the burger and a slice of tomato. Serve.

MODERN POT STICKERS

Ingredients for the dumplings
1 package of dumpling wrappers (almost all supermarkets carry them in the refrigerated section)
1 pound ground pork
1 bag of fresh arugula
1 minced garlic clove
1 minced shallot
1 green onion
1 pinch of salt
1 pinch of black pepper
2 tsp soy sauce

Ingredients for the dipping sauce
1 cup soy sauce
2 Tbsp sesame oil
1 finely chopped green onion
1/2 tsp finely chopped red chili (omit if you don't like spicy sauce)
1/2 tsp minced ginger

In a processor, mince the arugula with the garlic cloves, shallots, and green onion. Then move to a bowl with the ground pork and blend it all together thoroughly. Add 2 Tbsp of soy sauce, pinch of salt and pinch of black pepper.

On a dry cutting board, place a dumpling wrapper and put a teaspoon of the filling in the center. Dip your fingers in a bowl of cold water, then rub one-half of the wrapper with water and fold over the other half. Press down to seal. With the prongs of a fork, press around the rounded side that you just pressed down and seal them very well. Place on a plate that has been dusted with cornstarch until you have them all prepared and ready to be cooked.

In a frying pan, add 1/4 cup vegetable oil and heat over medium heat. When sizzling, add the dumplings and cook for about 4 minutes until they are brown on one side. Flip them over and add 1/2 cup of water and let them steam for another minute. They will be fried on one side and steamed on the other. Serve immediately with the dipping sauce.

MUSIC THAT INSPIRES ME

Here are some of my favorite go-to songs that help me move my brain into creativity mode. I'm not sure why they have that effect on me, but they do.

Can't Find My Way Home … Stevie Winwood

Brandy … Looking Glass

Hello … Adele

Yesterday … Beatles

Loose Yourself … Eminem

Gangsters Paradise … Coolio

The Alcott … The National w/ Taylor Swift

When Doves Cry … Prince

A Million Dreams … From the Greatest Showman

Come as You Are … Nirvana

In Da Club … 50 Cent

Sounds of Silence … Disturbed (instead of the Simon and Garfunkel version)

Once in a Lifetime … Talking Heads

Still Haven't Found What I'm Looking For … U2

In My Room … Beach Boys

BOOKS FOR WOULD-BE FILM MAKERS

The landscape of the entertainment world has changed in many ways, and these books provide good insight into how we got to where we are. Remember, though, that these are guides that provide historical perspective and are not a bible.

A Touch of the Madness by Larry Kasanoff: Larry is one of my favorite authors as he truly is a film maker who has been in the game successfully for several decades. He shares my thought that in order to have breakthrough hits, you need to think outside of the box and be a little crazy. If you want to learn from someone who has been involved in over 200 films, this is a must read.

In the Blink of an Eye by Walter Murch: A book about film editing from one of the true masters. Once you get in deep, you will realize that most of the great films or TV shows come together in the edit.

The Film Makers Handbook: A Comprehensive Guide for the Digital Age by Steven Ascher. A practical guide to just about all aspects of film making from pre to post and everything in between. A good read because it fully recognizes that we are in the digital age and that is not going away.

Story: Substance, Structure, Style and the Principles of Screenwriting by Robert McKee: a great guide to help you learn the basic rules from which you can develop your own style.

Rebel Without a Crew by Robert Rodriquez: Offers insight into indie filmmaking and chronicles the making of his first film.

Making Movies by Sidney Lumet: A great director's perspective on the craft of film making offering behind-the-scenes stories and practical advice.

Easy Riders, Raging Bulls: How the Sex, Drugs, and Rock and Roll Generation Saved Hollywood by Peter Biskind: This was actually one of the first books about Hollywood culture and dealings that I read, and it provided a historical perspective on what is called The New Hollywood Era and its impact on filmmaking.

Hitchcock/Truffaut by Frances Truffaut is a collection of interviews between Truffaut and Alfred Hitchcock, offering great insights into filmmaking techniques and directorial vision.

Adventures in The Screen Trade by William Goldman: A great screenwriter's candid perspective of the film industry.

The Five Cs of Cinematography: Motion Picture Filming by Joseph V. Mascelli is the classic guide to the art.

ABOUT LARRY J. NAMER

Larry J. Namer is an award-winning entertainment industry veteran with over five decades of professional experience in cable television, live experiences, and new media. Larry is an accomplished entrepreneur— notably, Mr. Namer is Founder of E! Entertainment Television, a cable network now valued at over five billion USD. E! is now in over 140 countries. His portfolio of successful media companies extends both domestically and internationally.

Namer's legacy is not only defined by his business ventures but also by his talent for discovering and nurturing emerging on-air personalities. His keen eye for talent has played a pivotal role in launching the careers of numerous individuals who have become synonymous with E!, such as Greg Kinnear, Howard Stern, and the Kardashians.

Namer's career began with a groundbreaking achievement: at a young age; he became the youngest general manager of a major cable system at Valley Cable TV (VCTV) in Los Angeles. Under his leadership, VCTV garnered numerous awards, including Emmy and Cable ACE nominations, and was recognized by *Forbes* magazine as a national model for local cable television programming.

His contributions to the industry have been acknowledged with many prestigious honors. Mr. Namer has been a recipient of the President's Award from the National Cable Television Association, and he was awarded The Tribeca Disruptor Award at the Novus Summit at the United Nations.

To learn more, visit www.ljnmedia.com.